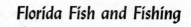

Florida Fish and Fishing

THE MACMILLAN COMPANY
NEW YORK · CHICAGO
DALLAS · ATLANTA · SAN FRANCISCO
LONDON · MANILA

**THE MACMILLAN COMPANY
OF CANADA, LIMITED**
TORONTO

FLORIDA FISH
and Fishing

by
PHIL FRANCIS

New York · The Macmillan Company · *1955*

For my wife Doris, a fishing widow with a rare and sympathetic understanding of her husband's fishing fever. Doris doesn't fish, but she sure types a mean manuscript on fishing.

The photographs in this book
were taken by the author.

Contents

vii

Introduction

IN WRITING a book about Florida fishing, it is most difficult
to present the facts in an interesting manner without making them sound like the glowing, flowery phrases of a chamber of commerce folder. Even in these days of polluted waters,
ruthless commercial exploitation, and tremendous fishing pressure almost everywhere, Florida's waters remain pure, and the
fishing pressure on them light. With some 30,000 named lakes
and 5,000 more without names, plus the longest coast line of
any state, Florida has water that (to use a Cracker expression)
"won't quit." Put all that water in a subtropical latitude, with
the Gulf of Mexico lapping at one side and the warm Gulf
Stream bordering the other, and you've got the makings of
an ideal situation for the production and maintenance of fish
life.

Still very much a tourist state, with little heavy industry,
Florida has no serious pollution problems, and its waters con-

tinue to produce fish much faster than any sport-fishing pressure can remove them. While there has been serious overfishing by salt-water commercial interests in certain areas, this situation is rapidly being corrected through restrictions on net sizes and types, as well as regulations prohibiting nets of all types in certain breeding grounds. All factors considered, Florida's fishing has suffered less as a result of civilization's inroads upon nature than any other state's.

This book is aimed at the average-guy type of fisherman —the local workingman who does his fishing on week ends, and the tourist who saves up all year for his fishing trip to Florida. Contrary to popular opinion, Florida fishing is as inexpensive as you'll find anywhere, and the average guy can have just as much—or more—fun as the fellow who ties his $25,000 yacht up to the dock of the hundred-dollar-per-day hotel. As a matter of fact, the millionaire angler would do well to get himself a skiff and try some of the light-tackle fishing described in these chapters. Chances are, he'd sell the yacht.

Sailfish and marlin are NOT for the average fisherman of modest means, except perhaps for an occasional splurge. For this reason, sailfish and marlin are not discussed in this book. And frankly—since I, too, am an average fisherman—I don't know enough about sailfishing or marlin fishing to discuss them intelligently. Tarpon, on the other hand, are definitely for the average fisherman; I've caught hundreds of them right off the river banks without spending even a dime for a skiff rental. Tarpon, therefore, are given a prominent place in the text.

This reasoning has been followed throughout these chapters. Each fish that receives space is within the reach of every reader. Since Florida waters are said to contain over 600 different species of fish, 100 of which are of some interest to the angler, it is possible that I've omitted a few. Nevertheless, you'll find all of the information you need on the most important species to catch them without too much difficulty. The others you'll catch by accident.

Much credit for this book is due George S. Fichter, former editor of *The Fisherman* magazine, who gave me the idea, did the preliminary leg work, and granted me permission to adapt material that first appeared under my by-line in *The Fisherman*. I also give my sincere thanks to Hugh Grey, who permitted me to include in these pages certain anecdotes from articles of mine in *Field & Stream;* and to Jim Mitchell, who permitted the use of anecdotes that had appeared in *Hunting & Fishing*. Thanks are due also to the many members of the Florida Outdoor Writers Association who shared their experience and hard-won knowledge with me, and thereby helped make this book possible. And last, but by no means least, may I say thanks to all of my long-suffering fishing partners, who have smilingly put up with my crazy experimenting and to-hell-with-supper attitude on many a fishing trip. A good fishing partner is a great asset, indeed a necessity to the angler who likes to experiment and eventually write a book.

CHAPTER 1

Salt-Water Spinning in Florida

Nот too many years ago, spinning in this country was little more than something spiders did to make webs. Not until after the last war did a few American anglers recognize spinning as a different way to take certain kinds of fresh-water fish—not a better way, but at least a different way. Now, in some of the coastal areas of the United States, spinning is rapidly becoming the most popular of all salt-water fishing methods—and incidentally, the most productive.

Along the New England coast, down through Long Island, New Jersey and the Chesapeake Bay area, spinning is winning new adherents as an angling method for bluefish, stripers, weakfish and other inshore feeders. In California, fishermen are taking spinning outfits out on the famous live-bait boats, and having more fun than they ever had before. But it is in Florida waters that spinning has been most enthusiastically received, for Florida has more kinds of lure-hitting fish than all the other states combined.

In the Keys, fishermen have found that the wily and hard-to-handle bonefish are suckers for spinning lures. On the Gulf coast, spin-casters are taking spotted weakfish in numbers that no other fishermen can match. Anglers who work the hard-fished waters of Biscayne Bay down Miami way are fooling cagey snappers and finicky pompano with spinning gear when even live shrimp fails to tempt these fish. Surf fishermen are roaming the ocean beaches in the Jacksonville area with spinning equipment, and catching big channel bass right out from under the noses of surfmen using conventional tackle and natural bait. The more adventurous spin-fishermen are taking their threadline gear offshore to the reefs and Gulf Stream and returning with dolphin, bonito, and a legion of other hard-fighting fishes of the open sea. Spinning's salt-water scope in Florida seems endless.

I didn't recognize spinning's full possibilities in salt water until I'd given the method a fairly long trial. The first fish I caught were small snook and jacks, common fish in Florida, and nothing to get excited about. I was impressed, however, with the strong fight these fish put up against the light spinning tackle. Then one day I sank the barb of my little bucktail hook into a big snook, a fourteen and one-half-pounder, and I was amazed at the smooth way the light rod and four-pound-test line handled him. As I branched out and fished different types of water, I began to realize that spinning tackle was not only giving me more fishing fun, but it was also getting me more fish than I had ever taken in salt water before. My casting and fly tackle seemed to develop severe short-comings, as spinning easily solved fishing problems for which my skill with the other methods was inadequate. Now I have reached the stage at which most veteran salt-water spin-casters eventually find themselves: I can no longer conceive of serious fishing in salt water without spinning tackle.

Probably the most appealing feature of salt-water spinning in Florida is the variety—the amazing variety—of fish species it takes on artificial lures. The first time I ever tried it in a salt-water area harboring many different kinds of fish, I came up with several species I'd never before taken on artificial lures, plus a few species that I'd never previously caught by any angling method.

That was the time Manny Eisfeld of Miami and I decided to try our relatively new spinning outfits on spotted sea trout near the mouth of the Caloosahatchee River, west of Fort Myers. We got the trout, all right, and before the day was over we had landed twenty-one other kinds of fish to boot, ranging from buck-toothed sheepshead to glamorous pompano. We got oddities like the rare coral mason, a little fish that builds itself a house out of bits of shell and coral; the remora, the hitch-hiking fish that attaches itself to large fish by means of suction cups; the porcupine fish, a spine-studded, small-mouthed nibbler we'd never expect to catch on an artificial lure. We jumped big tarpon, and lost them; and hooked big sharks, and lost them too. That was the day I began to realize the versatility of spinning. It seemed that the little bucktails we used appealed to every species of fish in the river.

Actually, Manny and I had a lot to learn at the time we made that first spectacular catch. We just happened to stumble upon ideal conditions and reckless fish. Had we known the tricks of lure manipulation and proper water coverage, there's no telling how many fish we'd have caught. Our beginner's luck was fortunate, however, as it gave us the confidence to stick with salt-water spinning and learn something about it.

There are certain techniques that may be used to great advantage in salt-water spinning. Simply casting out and reeling in does not produce more than a small fraction of the strikes to be had by proper manipulation of the lure. On the whole, salt-water fish are more manipulation conscious than their fresh-water cousins, and it really pays to know how to work a lure for them. This is why so many tourists are badly disappointed after their first try at Florida salt-water fishing.

The number one technique in salt-water spinning is that of bouncing the lure along the bottom. This is the secret of taking numerous species of fish that are not even considered to be strikers of artificial lures. The best lure for bottom-bouncing is a small weighted bucktail or nylon jig. I like the Upperman bucktail for this work, and I like the hair trimmed short. Even when trimmed short, bucktail has life and action that nylon or vinyl simply can't match. A shortened tail puts the hook in a strategic position for nailing many small-mouthed bottom feeders, which would strike short at an untrimmed lure. Trimming down bucktail in no way diminishes its appeal to striking fish; indeed the effect of making the lure smaller sometimes seems beneficial.

The technique of bouncing a bucktail jig along the bottom is simple. Just cast it out and allow it to sink all the way down. Now retrieve with a slow series of sharp whips of the rod tip, snapping the rod up suddenly and down again quickly so that the jig jumps off the bottom and settles right back. This will cause the lead head of the jig to dig into the sand or mud and raise a slight cloud as it does so. Strikes will usually come on the slack line between rod whips, as the fish scoop up the jig as it seems to be trying to bury itself in an attempt to get away from them. A jig bounced along the bottom so that it puffs up the sand will take several times as many fish as the same jig fished just off the bottom.

While we're on the subject of the bottom-bouncing and bottom-dragging methods of fishing a spinning jig, here's a tip on an excellent way to use these methods to locate fish—and to catch them. Allow your boat to drift with the wind or tide, and simply drag your jig along about thirty yards behind, bouncing it if you wish, or merely shaking the rod tip. All bait fishermen know and use drift methods, but most users of artificials overlook them. There is no better way to find bottom fish and to catch them with artificial lures.

A couple of years ago an old fishing buddy of mine from Maryland allowed me to sell him on a one-day fling at salt-water spinning in the Gulf of Mexico. I had laid it on pretty thick in building up this fishing, and my friend was well steamed up about bluefish, snook, ladyfish, jacks, mackerel, spotted weakfish and other near-surface feeders. When the big day arrived, however, a northwester was howling across the Gulf, and the situation seemed hopeless.

"Looks like we'll have to stick to sheltered water and concentrate on bottom fish, Bob," I remarked as we pulled out from the dock.

"Bottom fish!" he howled. "I didn't come all the way from Baltimore to catch bottom fish! Besides, we don't have any bait."

"Bottom fish aren't so bad," I said, "and you don't need bait to catch 'em with spinning tackle."

We began fishing in a natural channel along the lee shore of a little island, using small bucktail jigs with the hair trimmed short. Allowing the boat to drift along with the wind, we simply cast out behind and let the lures go to the bottom, working our rod tips slowly to give action to the bucktails.

Before we had drifted ten yards Bob gave a shout. "Boy, I've got one, and it's no bottom fish! Must be a snook or jack."

Bob's rod indeed testified that he "had one," and the drag on his reel sang again and again as the fish lunged and bored for bottom. Each time he managed to raise the fish a foot or two, it would fight back powerfully, and Bob would have to give ground. It was a real tug-of-war for a while, but Bob finally won and broke the fish to the surface. It wasn't a big fish, just a two-pound gag grouper, but Bob was all smiles as he picked up the landing net. "If this be bottom fishing," he quipped, "let's make the most of it."

And we did. Before calling it a day we had boated an interesting assortment of bottom fish, including whiting, grouper, snapper, drum, sandfish, channel bass, and a few specimens of that ultragame catfish, the gafftopsail. We even got a few spotted weakfish and ladyfish, which were down deep with the bottom species because of the bad weather. It was sporty, satisfying fishing, spiced with the suspense of wondering what the next fish would be.

"Spinning for bottom fish!" remarked Bob as he prepared to catch his plane back to Baltimore. "What will you Florida guys come up with next? I'm sure going to give it a try up home next summer."

I enjoy spinning for bottom fish even when I could just as easily go after bigger and more spectacular game, because when you sink a lure all the way to bottom in salt water, there's no telling what may latch on. Many fish that are not considered vulnerable to artificial lures are suckers for small spinning bucktails fished right on the bottom.

In addition to regular bottom fish, many of the species that ordinarily swim near the surface or in midwater some-times go deep. When fish like snook, jacks, and weakfish do go down, they're generally off their feed and not interested in any but the smallest of lures. Under these conditions, spinning bucktails fished deep will get 'em.

Fresh-water fly-fishermen have always been able to turn readily to bluegills, crappie, and other panfish when bass won't hit; but before spinning invaded these shores, salt-water arti-ficial-lure addicts were out of luck when the game species went into hiding. Since nearly all of the salt-water panfish are bottom feeders, lures small enough to tempt them couldn't be fished deep enough to reach them. Spinning for bottom fish has greatly increased the scope of the artificial-lure man in salt water.

The spin-caster holds an enormous advantage over the bait-caster and fly-fisherman when it comes to taking deep-feeding fish on artificial lures. The fly rod, of course, is suitable only for surface and near-surface fishing. The bait-casting rod is OK for deep fishing, all right, but not with the light, com-pact lures that are so appealing to most bottom fish. Spinning, on the other hand, allows the use of small but fast-sinking weighted bucktails and jigs, with every chance of success with such bottom-hugging fish as flounders, croakers, whiting, grouper, porgies, grunts, and many others.

Many of Florida's lesser-known salt-water fish are grub-bers with small mouths designed for picking food right off the bottom, and they do most of their feeding on shellfish—either mollusks, or crustaceans, or both. To catch such feeders con-

sistently with artificial lures, you must keep this fact in mind
and try to make your lures behave accordingly. It goes without saying that the lure must be fished right on the bottom,
for bottom fish in general will ignore lures that pass above
them.

One winter when Joe Bauer was down here in Florida
looking for fish and fish stories, I gave him a terrific propa-
gandizing on the merits of spinning in salt water. We arranged
a trip to Punta Rassa, where the Caloosahatchee River meets
the Gulf of Mexico. Nearly all day long we did little but cast,
and change lures, and catch an occasional spotted weakfish.
Joe was politely tolerant of the slow fishing, but I was really
sweating out my reputation as a conservative liar. Finally I
struck on the idea of deep-drift fishing with Upperman bucktails through one of the navigation channels, and that saved the
day. In less than an hour we had caught two dozen sand weakfish (a relatively uncommon deep-swimming species indigenous to the Gulf of Mexico), plus an assortment of bottom
panfish. Joe is now a confirmed salt-water spinner.

In a fast tide, spinning jigs and bucktails also work very
well when fished "dead," as nymphs and wet flies are sometimes
fished for Northern stream trout. The cast is made across the
tide, and the lure is allowed to be swept in an arc until it is
straight downtide from the angler. Then it is retrieved slowly,
with a darting action imparted by the rod. The lighter bucktails in the one-eighth-ounce class are in order for this fishing,
but in deep water, heavier lures may be needed. This is a killing
technique for snapper especially, and produces well with snook
and sea trout.

Most salt-water fish like a straight, darting action rather
than the wiggles and wobbles preferred by fresh-water species.

For this reason no other lures are so consistently successful as jigs and bucktails in salt water. Bucktail or nylon jigs are adaptable to a number of fishing techniques, the simplest of which involves no more than casting out and retrieving with a whipping rod motion. The speed of the retrieve is easily varied, and the rod whips may be short or long, making possible almost infinite diversity. Because of the great number of ways spinning bucktails may be worked, these lures will nearly always take fish if anything will.

A trick that has worked wonders for me on many Florida spinning trips is the use of two lures at a time. Bill Upperman, the bucktail man of Atlantic City, New Jersey, gets the credit for this one—at least it was Bill who first mentioned it to me. When the fish want a small lure, but the tide and water depth prevent getting it down to them, use two small lures! Why use a sinker, which provides nothing but dead weight, when another lure can give the weight you need to get down, and can furnish an added attraction to boot? By using two jigs of slightly different style or color, you can get needed weight for deep fishing while keeping the size of the lure small; determine quickly which style and color the fish prefer; and make many double catches. Even when the extra weight is not needed, I find that two jigs usually produce better than one. Once you hook a fish on one of the jigs, his schoolmates find it hard to resist the other one, and this makes for a barrel of fun with light spinning gear. Then, too, for reasons I don't pretend to know, two jigs of the same pattern in tandem seem to draw more strikes than a single one—even in shallow, still water where the extra weight is not needed. The use of two flies is old stuff to trout fishermen, and most salt-water anglers

employ two baited hooks as routine practice. Try two spinning bucktails sometime, in either fresh or salt water.

The most practical way I've found to rig two jigs is to
use an eighteen-inch length of nylon leader material for the
trailer jig and a nine-inch wire leader for the first jig. Tie a
snap to one end of the nylon and the jig on the other. This rig
is easily attached by inserting the snap through the lower eye
of the leader swivel, and it is readily detached if you wish to
return to a single lure. The swivel does a swell job of keeping
the nylon and wire free of tangles.

Although not so consistent as bucktails and jigs, most of
the standard fresh-water spinning lures will take salt-water
fish, and at times they produce even better than lures designed
for salt water. The miniature plugs in one-eighth- and one-
fourth-ounce sizes are acceptable to weakfish, bluefish, snook,
barracuda, jacks, and some of the other more common Florida
species. Generally speaking, the surface types, like the darters,
injured minnows, and plunkers, are more valuable in salt water
than the underwater plugs with metal tips to make them
wiggle. When subsurface lures are called for, bucktails and
spoons are apt to produce much better than plugs. Be that as
it may, salt water fish are unpredictable, and there are times
when the tiny underwater plugs work wonders.

Spinning plugs are retrieved in exactly the same manner
as their casting-size counterparts, but any plug works best in
salt water when moved more rapidly than it would be in fresh
water. At times it pays to fairly skitter a top-water lure across
the surface, keeping the rod tip whipping all the while. Many
salt-water fish are excited into striking by such a retrieve, the
snook, bluefish, channel bass, and tarpon, for example.

A large assortment of lures is not necessary to Florida salt-water spinning success. Learning how to use the few basic types I have mentioned is much more sensible than collecting all the colors and styles you can find. A few yellow, white, and red-and-white jigs and plugs, and silver or copper spoons in spinning sizes, will give you about as versatile an inventory of lures as you can handle.

At one time I had become so enthusiastic about spinning's great versatility that I honestly didn't think there was anything I couldn't do with it in salt water. Then one day, when fishing off Fort Myers with a couple of bait-casting buddies, I was jolted with the realization that there *are* fishing situations with which spinning tackle cannot cope. One of my whippy retrieves was interrupted by a sharp strike, and I nonchalantly set the hook and turned to my friends.

"When are you guys going to get some tackle that will catch fish?" I asked.

At that instant there was a tremendous commotion in the water, and my reel broke into a high whine. A huge dark form exploded out of the water and crashed back down with a terrifying splash. I had hooked a giant manta ray, which looked to be ten feet across the back! My line was going fast, so I automatically started the motor to follow the big ray. Before I could get my bearings the boat had run aground on an oyster bar, and there was nothing to do but tighten the drag and break the line.

"I guess that will shut you up for a while," one of my companions remarked.

Tales I'd heard of all-day fights with harpooned mantas came into my mind, and I had to laugh as I looked at my tiny rod and four-pound-test line. "Yes," I agreed, "I guess it will. Spinning has its limitations, all right."

While there are a number of spinning rods and reels made especially for salt-water fishing; most of them are larger and heavier than necessary. I feel that spinning tackle—or any tackle—for salt water should be light enough to give sport with the *average* fish encountered, not heavy enough for the biggest fish in the sea. And, even in Florida, the average fish encountered is modest in size.

Indeed, fresh-water-type equipment—if the hardware is corrosion-proof—will give more pleasure per fish than heavy spinning gear, and will pay additional dividends in numbers and variety of fish caught. The inherent lightness of spinning tackle is directly responsible for its success, and it is foolish to sacrifice this for power that may never be needed anyway. A big spinning outfit is fine for some purposes, but a light one is more versatile.

A hollow glass rod, about six and one-half feet long and weighing four to four and one-half ounces is best for all-around use. The rod should have some backbone, for the buggy-whip rod action is useless for salt-water spinning. The trend these days is towards fast tip action with stiffness in the lower part of the rod, as in the Sila-Flex reinforced-butt models. This arrangement provides power where it is needed, without sacrificing ability to cast light lures.

Guides and ferrules should be of corrosion-resistant material, preferably chrome-plated stainless steel or Monel. Many spin-casters like a screw-locking reel seat on their salt-water spinning rods, as the plain cork handle with reel bands is said sometimes to allow the reel to work loose during a long fight. I personally have never experienced this alleged shortcoming, even in battles lasting more than an hour, but there is no question that a screw-locking reel seat is more positive than reel bands.

The spinning reel for salt-water use should be selected with care. Many reels that give good service in fresh water simply will not stand the combined onslaughts of salt-water corrosion and salt-water fish. Florida conditions of sun, salt, and humidity are especially hard on reels. Fortunately, manufacturers, both domestic and foreign, have recognized the need for ruggedness and corrosion resistance in spinning reels, and the latest models of several makes hold up fairly well. The Centaure and Orvis reels deserve special mention for their outstanding resistance to salt water.

Particular attention should be given to the pickup and line-roller mechanism of a spinning reel. The pickup bail or finger (either style is satisfactory) should be of stainless steel or Monel. The "roller," which may or may not actually roll, will wear a line at a terrific rate if it becomes worn or corroded. It therefore must be hard enough to resist grooving, as well as impervious to the chemical action of salt water. Carbaloy, *genuine* agate, and hard stainless steel are the most satisfactory materials for rollers. Reels with stationary rollers should be designed so that the roller may be turned when one side becomes grooved, and easily replaced when worn on all sides.

A fast-retrieving reel is needed in salt water, not only for working lures, but also for fighting fast fish. The gear ratio alone does not determine the speed of retrieve, but merely the number of pickup revolutions per turn of the handle. Spool diameters vary considerably, and a big spool will take up line much faster than a small one on a given ratio. Most spinning reel makers state the length of line retrieved per revolution of the handle, and this figure should be about twenty-two inches or greater for salt-water fishing. One of my favorites, a large but lightweight reel, zips line in at a rate of over thirty inches per turn of the handle.

Be sure that the spinning reel you choose for salt-water use has a smooth, dependable drag, because you're certainly going to need it. The drag nut should tighten gradually, so that slight adjustments may be made without danger of applying too much or too little tension. A reel offering at least two full turns of the wing nut from free to locked spool will allow fine adjustments of the drag, even with a fish on.

An antireverse lock is an absolute necessity on a spinning reel, and practically all makes now have this feature. Spools must be strong enough to stand the crushing pressure of elastic monofilament nylon lines. I have seen many plastic spools split when rugged salt-water fish were being worked in after long runs. Aluminum and stainless steel spools seem to have what it takes.

Don't be afraid to use plenty of oil and grease on a spinning reel, especially in salt water. Liberal lubrication will not slow a spinning reel down one bit, but will greatly reduce salt-water damage.

To my way of thinking there is nothing to compare with monofilament nylon for spinning lines. DuPont Tynex, a soft nylon, really makes a wonderful monofilament line. Monofilamet nylon wears much longer and casts better than braided lines of equal strength. It is practically invisible in the water. It does not become soggy and stick to itself, even after many hours of continuous casting in sticky salt water.

Probably the most useful size of monofilament nylon for salt water is six-pound test. The average reel will hold about

200 yards of this size, and in DuPont Tynex, it will cast lures as light as one-tenth ounce satisfactorily and handle lures as heavy as one-half ounce with safety. Do not make the mistake of trying to use too heavy a line, for doing so would defeat the very purpose of spinning.

For fishing around pilings, oyster beds, mangroves, and the like, carry an extra spool with seven- or eight-pound line on it. But stick to six-pound test or smaller where there is room to let your fish run. For large salt-water spinning reels and big, six- to eight-ounce rods, lines of eight- to twelve-pound test can be used to cast fairly large lures, but such tackle will not take nearly so many fish as the light, fresh-water-size gear.

It pays to use a wire leader when salt-water fishing in Florida. I personally prefer the light, braided stainless steel, but size 2 stainless music wire is also good. Many of Florida's salt-water fish are well fixed for teeth, hard gums, or other line-cutting facilities, and they make short work of spinning lines unless leaders provide protection. Use a size 12 swivel at one end and size 2 snap on the other.

Salt-water spinning in Florida will be a revelation to any fisherman trying it for the first time. Nearly all salt-water fish will strike artificial spinning lures, and many of them actually seem to prefer spinning lures to natural bait. By using the lures and tactics described in this section, anyone can catch plenty of hard-fighting Florida fish. At this writing, I have landed a total of eighty-nine different species of salt-water fish in Florida, all on spinning tackle and all on one make of artificial lure. The key lure is the small Upperman bucktail. Sink it deep to open the door to a vast volume of new and fantastic adventures in fishing.

CHAPTER 2

His Majesty, the Tarpon

H AVE you ever had to climb a tree to retrieve your lure—with a fish attached? Have you ever had the experience of trying to control a sizzling run downstream, then suddenly finding it necessary to duck to keep your fish out of your face? Did you ever see a fish bounce four feet after hitting the water from a two-foot jump? Have you ever felt a fish rubbing his hook-snagged jaw along the bottom of a ten-foot-deep pool while you watched him shaking and twisting in the air? No, I'm not a psychiatrist probing for hallucinations—just wondered if you've ever fished for tarpon. If you cannot answer any of the above questions in the affirmative, you've missed the most maddening, the wackiest, the most interesting, the roughest, the most spectacular—well, the best gol durned fishing the U. S. A. has to offer!

One summer a Maryland friend of mine accompanied me to the Imperial River on Florida's lower west coast for his orientation in fly-fishing for small tarpon. Al was a pretty handy guy with a fly rod on such staid Northern performers as trout and bass, but I wasn't too sure that he was damfool enough to get along with tarpon.

"Do tarpon fight much differently than bass?" Al asked.

"Yeah," I said. "Much differently."

We loaded our gear in a skiff and putted a short distance down river. There were the tarpon, rolling lazily in midstream.

"There they are, Al," I shouted as I cut the motor. "Start casting!"

Al was pretty nervous and excited, but he managed to get his popper out a few feet from the boat. A five-pound tarpon caught the bug as it hit the water, simultaneously catapulted himself into a tremendous leap that sent him crashing into Al's chest, then bounced back into the water. So shaken was Al, mentally as well as physically, that several seconds passed before he realized that he had lost the fish.

"Holy cow!" Al stammered. "Do they always do that?"

I tried to appear imperturbed. "Not always," I said, "only when they feel a hook. Take your fly off your shirt and start casting."

"You cast," Al said. "I'll watch."

"No, go ahead, Al, this is your party," I told him. "Get your bug far enough away from the boat to give them room to jump."

Muttering something about liking to fish as relaxation, not as a means to a violent end, Al reluctantly resumed casting. Relieved when his fly was undisturbed for the first few retrieves, he calmed down and managed to lengthen his casts. He nicked a tarpon and held him for one very moderate jump.

Then another. The next one latched on solidly and was firmly hooked.

"That one's nice fly size, Al, about seven pounds. I'll keep the boat away from him; you just hold on and give him all the pressure your rod can take," I said.

After ten minutes the tarpon was still hooked and had given up jumping for a deep, plodding fight. Al made the fish work for every wave of its fins, and soon the tarpon showed definite signs of tiring.

"If I land him I'm going to have him mounted," Al remarked. "He's just the right size for a trophy."

Eighteen minutes from the time of the strike, the tarpon was lying on his side at the water's surface, about ten or twelve feet from my position in the stern of the boat.

"He's through, Al," I said. "Reel . . ."

That was as far as I got. A shimmering flash of silver appeared in my face, and I instinctively ducked as low as possible. The tarpon soared over my head, thudded into the bottom of the boat, and lay still.

"Holy cow, holy cow, holy cow," Al was muttering.

"Well, that's one way to land 'em," I managed. "I'll unhook him for you."

"You don't have to," Al said. "There's my bug out in the water where he jumped!"

In his crass efforts to meet his doom in a blaze of glory, (and maybe take an angler with him) the spunky little tarpon had missed his chance for freedom!

Like all practical jokers, tarpon sometimes go too far and find that the joke is on them; or for all I know their anything-for-a-laugh philosophy may lead them purposely to perpetrate exhibitionistic tricks at their own expense.

You'd think that an aristocratic, graceful, and highly respected fish like the tarpon would be dignified, modest, and of refined sensibilities. At the very least, you'd expect the tarpon to conduct himself in a manner befitting his regal title of Silver King. The tarpon, however, is a vulgar, tactless, and clownish fish with a perverted and garish sense of humor.

Don't get me wrong. On tarpon, vulgarity, clownishness, and a perversely garish sense of humor look good. Tarpon wouldn't be tarpon if they didn't do the things they do, and fishing for them might be a tame, conventional type of angling if they weren't such unrestrained exhibitionists. Tarpon are great because they're eccentric, and can afford to be eccentric because they're great.

I've often wondered whether tarpon get together with other tarpon and hash over the good times they've had playing nasty tricks on fishermen. Every time a tarpon throws a plug full of hooks into my face, my mind's eye pictures him swimming back to the school and telling his buddies—probably with embellishments—what he did to me, reveling in the coarse laughter his story evokes. Maybe my imagination does get a little out of hand at times, but there's no getting around the fact that tarpon are the practical jokers of fishdom, and that some of their pranks border on the diabolical. It is certain that few anglers are temperamentally capable of putting up with them long enough to become really *good* tarpon fishermen.

To be a good tarpon fisherman it has been said that you don't have to be crazy, but it helps. I take issue with this statement on the grounds that the process of becoming a good tarpon fisherman is bound to drive you crazy; therefore, a *good* tarpon fisherman is necessarily a crazy one. While the reverse is by no means true, it must be admitted that crazy people learn to become good tarpon fishermen much more quickly than noncrazy ones. Also requisite to becoming a good tarpon fisherman are an unusually good sense of humor and a devil-may-care attitude about things. Tarpon can drive rational persons insane, scare cautious persons out of their wits, and throw ill-humored persons into vitriolic fits of frustrated rage. Should you feel that you do not have the emotional requirements for becoming a good tarpon fisherman, don't let that stop your fishing for them; for if you can manage to put up with them, tarpon will provide you with more to talk about than all other fish combined. To put up with them, just refuse to take them seriously, and you'll get along fine. Be prepared for anything, for when you attempt to sink a hook into brother tarpon's ironclad jaw, anything is liable to happen.

One September day I was standing on the railroad bridge that spans Florida's Caloosahatchee River at Goodno, catching a smoke and watching C. J. Nielsen's futile attempts to coax a strike out of a furiously feeding tarpon. The tarpon, a four-footer, was dining directly under the bridge on small minnows and making all sorts of uncouth eating noises as he gulped them down.

C. J. stood on the bank and made cast after cast with lure after lure, but the tarpon went right on with his minnow-slurping as though C. J.'s lures didn't exist. Soon C. J. began making uncouth noises too, but they could hardly be classified as eating noises. When he had made at least fifty fruitless casts with his favorite feather jig, I felt that the time had arrived to give C. J. a bit of a ribbing.

"What's the matter," I taunted. "Don't you know how to work a feather for tarpon?"

"I know how to work the feather," C. J. barked. "That tarpon just doesn't know a good retrieve when he sees it!"

"Whip it," I suggested.

"What do you think I've been doing, swatting mosquitoes with my rod?" he demanded.

A sudden silly whim prompted me to drop my feather between the railroad ties and allow the reel to feed line until the lure hit the water. For the next few seconds the air under the bridge seemed to be filled with flying tarpon, and the water boiled and exploded and disintegrated into clouds of spray. Then all was quiet, and I groggily reeled up a broken line.

"I've heard of lots of ways to fish a feather, but that's a new one," said C. J. "What did you do, thread it through a bolt hole?"

That tarpon knew what he was doing. Tarpon do similar things far too often for happenstance. He wouldn't hit C. J.'s feather because C. J.'s position on the bank was favorably suited for playing a fish. But when he saw my feather descend through the railroad ties, he just couldn't resist having some fun with me. He had it, and I wouldn't especially mind—if C. J. would only stop referring to me as the guy who fishes for tarpon through bolt holes. People might get funny ideas.

Tarpon have put me up a tree many times, usually figuratively, but on one occasion, literally! Now I have never been much of a hand for tree-climbing, being content to leave such monkeyshines to the monkeys. If, however, I should take a notion to climb a tree, I'd select an oak, maple, or preferably a fruit-laden apple or cherry tree. Never a mangrove. Tree-scaling people who know their trees contend that the mangrove is among the least desirable of trees for climbing. Having climbed a mangrove, I can fully appreciate their low regard for it. Mangrove-climbing is at best a degrading experience, especially when it is accomplished within full view of a busy thoroughfare on a Sunday afternoon.

On a particular Sunday afternoon a couple of years ago I was fly-casting for baby tarpon from a small bridge on the highway between Fort Myers and Fort Myers Beach. The fish were hitting well, and a sizable audience of Sunday drivers had congregated to watch me do my stuff. Feeling a bit hammy, I polished up my casting form and assumed what I considered to be the attitude of an efficient tarpon fly-fisher. The tarpon seemed to be in a show-offy mood too, for a mere nick of the hook would send them into frenzied, unusually high leaps. Finally the hook stuck solidly in a two-footer, and he outdid himself. He landed in the outer branches of a mangrove tree, six feet above the water level, and stayed there. I couldn't pull him down, because he had taken the precaution of tangling the line among the branches.

"Shake him out," somebody suggested.

I tried it. I shook and shook, but all I could shake out of that mangrove was a horde of famished mosquitoes and sand flies.

"Why don't you break the line?" asked an observer.

"Mister, ten-dollar fly lines don't grow on trees!" I snapped.

"Yours does," was his maddening reply. "All you have to do is climb the tree and pick it."

So I climbed the mangrove tree. I climbed the tree before an audience of cheering and jeering Sunday drivers, my ears ringing with the buzz of mosquitoes, the advisory remarks of the spectators, and the squeal of tires and brakes as more drivers stopped to see "the guy who's climbing a tree after a tarpon." Just as I stretched out a hand for the tarpon, he gave a flip and plunged down through the branches into the water, leaving the fly in the tree.

"Oh! You lost him!" some sympathetic onlooker observed.

"Did he get away?" asked another.

"I released him!" I lied through clenched teeth. "I always release tarpon."

I finally got my line untangled from the branches and picked my way back down to the ground, mosquito-riddled and mortified, and wanting no more tarpon fishing that day. As I loaded myself and my fly rod into the car, the voice of a little girl deftly applied the finishing touch to my humiliation.

"Mommie, isn't the man going to climb the tree any more?"

When this incident occurred, I had not yet acquired the devil-may-care attitude that tarpon fishermen must have. In retrospect, I feel that the impish little tarpon let me off easy. Most mangrove trees have wasps' nests in them.

Playful devilishness among tarpon isn't confined to the little ones by any means. The big, barrel-chested silver kings over six feet long are every bit as impish as the little ones, but they are less numerous and therefore have less opportunity to jest with the angler.

Big tarpon are at their best as pranksters when you're not fishing for them or do not suspect that one of them is anywhere near. At such times they like to sneak up on you and send you home to blubber in your beer.

C. J. Nielsen and I were snook fishing in the Caloosahatchee River one evening after having spent most of the

afternoon at a spot farther downriver, trying without success
to tempt members of a school of large tarpon with live catfish
at the end of regulation 6/9 outfits. We had given up on the
tarpon and were now enjoying a relaxing change of pace with
light glass casting rods rigged with fresh-water reels full of
ten-pound-test line. Our tackle was just right for the three- to
five-pound snook we were catching, the weather was pleasant
as only South Florida weather can be, and there seemed to be
no tarpon around to take our minds off the peaceful sport at
hand, or our eyes off the beautiful sunset.

Suddenly the calm silence was rudely interrupted by a
boisterous splash, which made me think that C. J., a two-
hundred-pounder, had fallen overboard.

"Was that you, C. J.?" I called.

"You know I never mix fishing and swimming," he said.
"There, in the middle of the river. Big tarpon."

I walked over to where C. J. was standing and we
watched the widening circles for further signs of the fish. As
we watched, a huge head broke the surface, and fully seven
feet of tarpon followed it in a leisurely roll.

"Wow!" I exclaimed. "That's the biggest tarpon I've ever
seen. He'll go two hundred pounds."

"Easy that," C. J. agreed.

Snook fishing operations were called off right then and
there while we made a mad dash to the car for the 6/9 outfits
and live catfish. With hands full of thumbs we managed to
string up the rods, tie on leaders and hooks, impale catfish baits
and make casts. We'd cast the catfish out, allow them to swim
to the bottom as catfish will, and then retrieve slowly. For ten
or fifteen minutes we put our casts all over that section of the
river, but the big tarpon had apparently moved on.

"To heck with him," I said. "I'm going to get another snook."

Picking up my casting rod I attempted a long cast with a small feather jig. The line backlashed. It was a bad one, so I sat down to relax while picking it out. C. J., meanwhile, kept after the big tarpon with his live catfish. Finally I got the backlash out, and when I started to reel in the jig, I found that it had evidently fouled on bottom. I whipped the rod, plucked at the line, and walked up and down the bank to try from every angle to loosen it, but the jig stayed put.

"Guess I'll have to break it," I said. Wrapping my handkerchief around my hand to avoid being cut by the thin line, I took a couple of turns of the line about the handkerchief and pulled. Suddenly the line was moving! Before I could get it off my hand it had broken, and at the same instant the seven-foot tarpon came out of the water in a mighty leap with my feather jig in his mouth. Tarpon do the darndest things!

Probably the most maddening tarpon I've ever run into was the one Manny Eisfeld of Miami hooked near Shell Island in the lower Caloosahatchee River. Manny and I were drifting slowly in a skiff and casting ahead of the boat with spinning tackle when I caught a small silver perch.

"Let me have him," Manny said. "I'll put him on the big outfit and let him drag behind the boat for cobia."

The "big outfit" consisted of a light, hollow glass boat rod and a large level-winding star-drag reel full of twenty-five-pound-test squidding line. Manny looped on a five-foot steel leader and 8/o hook, baited with the live perch, and cast it out behind the boat. He left the reel in free spool, engaged the click, and, after placing the rod in a secure position in the boat, resumed casting with his spinning gear.

We hadn't drifted very far when the click began to sing and the boat rod started hopping. Throwing me his spinning rod and picking up the boat rod, Manny slammed the reel in gear and leaned into the fish hard. Out came a tarpon, a six-foot tarpon that looked as wide as an orange crate.

"Take the rod, Phil; you like these darn things!" Manny exclaimed. "I don't want any part of him in this little skiff."

"Nothing doing," I said. "It's your fish. Pour it to him and make him jump."

Manny again leaned back on the rod, and again the tarpon came to the surface, beating the water to a froth as he walked about on his broad tail.

"Phil, if you don't take this rod I'm going to break him off. I don't mind telling you I'm scared to death of tarpon this size."

Manny sounded serious, so I consented to take over. "There's no danger, Manny," I said. "Watch me tame him down."

I tightened the star drag a little and began pumping the fish. Strangely enough, it didn't take much pumping, for the big tarpon offered just enough resistance to keep the line tight. I kept reeling, and before I woke up to what was happening I had the tarpon right where he wanted me: under the skiff.

"Are you crazy?" Manny shouted. "Get that fish out of here!"

It *was* a ticklish situation. "If you've got any suggestions, I'll listen to them," I said. "Maybe if I slacken the line he'll go away."

I let the line go slack, and we just sat there for a few minutes. The chummy tarpon, however, seemed perfectly content to remain in the cool shade of our little boat. With sudden inspiration I started the outboard motor. "We'll run away from him, Manny," I said.

Sure enough, the tarpon moved out from under the boat. I gunned the motor to get away from him, throwing the reel in free spool so as not to put any tension on him until we were at a safe distance. We had traveled about fifty yards when I noticed that the line was not straight behind the boat, but bellied out in a long U as if the hook were hung in the stern. Slowing the motor, I cautiously reeled in the slack and tightened up on the line. The tarpon was still on, swimming contentedly along right in the wash of the propeller.

"You sure tamed him, all right," Manny said. "Just like Mary's little lamb."

I was getting worried. "This is serious," I said. "That tarpon is green. If he decides to go into his dance he's liable to come into the boat and kick us out."

I tried speeding up the motor again, this time with the reel in gear, hoping to make the fish start jumping and to run out from under him. Evidently the tarpon guessed what I was up to, for he merely continued to tag along, increasing his speed to match the boat's pace. For a quarter of a mile the tarpon paced us; I could not get the boat away from him.

"Cut the line," Manny ordered.

"Nothing doing! I've never cut a fish off in my life, and I don't intend to start now," I said. "I'll get him away from the boat somehow."

Finally, as we passed a channel-marker, the rod came to life and the tarpon started to run. I cut the motor and settled down to the business of whipping the big silver king, pumping the rod vigorously to irritate him into jumping away some of his energy. But the tarpon had other ideas. He easily made the thirty yards to the channel-marker, swung around it, and it was all over.

Maybe it *was* a coincidence, but I sincerely believe that the tag-along tarpon had purposely bided his time until a fool-proof chance for escape presented itself. He probably figured that we'd pass some sort of line-snagging device if he held out long enough, so he saved his energy for the right tactical moment.

Tarpon delight in making anglers suffer, either mentally, or physically, or both, if they can so manage. Their most common procedure of torment is to grab your plug, hold it for an opportune moment, and then try to fling it in your face. Just knowing what a hooked tarpon intends to try to do with your plug provides anxiety enough for any fisherman, but when he has actually sent a plug whizzing past your ear a couple of times you come to understand what real mental agony can be. Then, his aim is occasionally true and the pain becomes intensely physical, as many tarpon anglers—including this one —can attest.

Once in a while you'll run into a tarpon with more imaginative ideas for the crucifixion of anglers. Like the one C. J. and I met in the Imperial River one day.

It was one of those hot, steamy, windless days that I'm happy to say are rare in South Florida. The June sun fairly sizzled the sweat on our backs. Boy, was it hot! And we had no drinking water along. It was back at camp in the car, four miles up the river.

Fishing was good that day, with snook, jacks, and spotted sea trout walloping our plugs and flies lustily. In the face of such fast sport, we couldn't bring ourselves to go back for the water jug until the demands of thirst became almost unbearable. Finally we felt that we just couldn't hold out any longer.

"Let's go get the water," C. J. said. "It's a half-hour's run up to the car, and I'm not even sure I can last that long."

"Right," I said. "Let's go!"

I made one last cast with the fly rod and began to reel in the line. Something grabbed the fly, skittered across the surface of the water like a planing speedboat, then hurled itself into the air in a high, twisting jump.

"Tarpon!" I shouted. "The first one I've seen today!"

"Break him off!" C. J. demanded. "Let's get that water."

"No," I said, "it won't take long; he's not very big. Take the paddle and keep the boat out from the shore for me."

Knowing me for a tarpon nut, C. J. resignedly picked up the paddle and kept the boat under control. Evidently, the hot sun was too much for the tarpon, for he refused to come out of the water again after that first jump. His fight settled down to a series of short, relatively slow runs. Back and forth he swam, calmly, but with irresistible determination. I leaned back on the rod, tapped the reel seat, and plucked at the taut line with my fingers, trying to sting the tarpon and make him jump, but he ignored my proddings.

"Ten minutes," C. J. announced. "Make him jump. I'm thirsty!"

"He won't last much longer," I said. "Look at the pressure I'm putting on him."

After a long period of silence during which I had begun to hold my fly rod with both hands in order to bring more pressure to bear on the tarpon, C. J. spoke again.

"Twenty minutes," he said. "Break him off."

"I can't break him off now, not after spending this much time on him," I said, wiping the sweat out of my eyes.

Another long period of silence, interrupted by no sounds except the gentle swish of the line as the tarpon continued his plodding runs.

"Thirty minutes," C. J. whispered hoarsely. "We could have been drinking that cool water by now."

"Yeah," I said, "I'll get him soon."

More silence.

"Forty minutes," C. J.'s voice sounded far away.

I acknowledged the information with a nod, too thirsty to speak. The tarpon plodded on, and on, and on. My wrist began to ache.

C. J. held up his hands and spread his fingers five times. Fifty minutes! The tarpon doggedly refused to give ground. Then he faltered. The pressure of the bamboo brought him out of a boring run and rolled him to the surface. Again he tried to break into a run, and again the rod pressure was too much for him. He made a half-hearted attempt to jump, then lay on his side exhausted. I stuck my thumb in his mouth and hoisted him aboard.

"Fifty-seven minutes," C. J. croaked as he prepared to start the motor. "What's he weigh?"

The pocket scales said six pounds. I passed the information along to C. J. and released the fish.

C. J. shook his head slowly. He started to say something, but changed his mind and started the motor instead.

Later, when we were sitting in the shade gargling nectar-like ice water, I remarked that the tarpon had set a new endurance record for fish I'd caught on a minutes-of-fight-per-pound-of-fish basis. His nine and one-half minutes of fight per pound had beaten my previous record of six minutes per pound set by a jack crevalle.

"That was the toughest tarpon I ever saw," I said. "My wrists and hands will never be the same."

"No, I don't think he was overly tough," said C. J. "He was probably just an ordinary tarpon with a particularly vicious sense of humor—and somehow he found out how thirsty we were."

If you haven't done much tarpon fishing you may think that C. J.'s remark was either facetious or downright silly, but experienced tarpon fishermen will recognize the sound wisdom behind it. Tarpon have an uncanny ability to detect an angler's weakness, and they'll go to any lengths to take every advantage of it. If they can't drive you mad, they'll try to scare you to death. If you are of fearless nature, they'll attempt to do you bodily harm. Should you be lucky enough to escape being injured by flying plugs, a swamped boat, or powerfully flailing tarpon tails, they'll still find a way to make you suffer. But they'll make you like the suffering. They may offend you with their hooligan tactics, destroy your dignity as a human being, discredit you as an angler, shock you by their impudence, terrify you or even cause you physical pain with their vehement fighting fury; but you'll like it. You'll like it, not in spite of your mental and physical tortures, but because of them. You'll like it because the things tarpon do to you will remain sharply etched in your mind when all other angling memories have faded. You'll like it because you cannot avoid realization that these crazy, boisterous, flashily clad jitterbugs that do the wildest things are ultragame—the scrappiest creatures on fins.

Is is customary, in evaluating the gameness of a fish, to give full consideration to the size of the fish, following the precedent of Dr. Henshall's inch-for-inch and pound-for-pound qualification in calling the black bass the gamest fish. This taking-size-into-account method of rating game fish is fair, perhaps, to the fish, but it is decidedly unfair to the angler.

The little bluegill fights hard for his size, true, but he would fight much harder if his average weight were five pounds instead of eight ounces. Many of the smaller fishes are spunky scrappers, but they simply do not have enough weight to stage a serious assault upon the fisherman's tackle. In the prize ring a good little man hasn't a chance against a good big man. On hook and line a good big fish fights with considerably more authority than a good little one.

The tarpon may or may not be the "gamest" fish on an inch-for-inch, pound-for-pound basis. Who can say? All anyone can do with such a question is to express a personal opinion. There is no standard measuring stick by which the gameness of fishes can be determined. For that matter, there exists a very wide diversity of opinion as to what constitutes gameness in a fish.

Few will deny that the tarpon as a jumper is in a class by himself. His jumps are more than mere leaps out of the water. They are wild, twisting, shimmering, hell-for-leather flights into the atmosphere. Perhaps the king mackerel manages occasionally to jump higher than the tarpon, and the marlins may jump wider, but no other fish jumps so handsomely. No other fish cuts so great a swath of air as the acrobatic silver king. No other fish hurls itself into its leaps with such an explosive abandon or with so great an expenditure of energy. The tarpon summersaults, spins, swaps ends, and shakes his head violently from the time he leaves the water until gravity sends him crashing back into it.

The tarpon's supremacy as a leaper is attested by the

familiar simile that has been used hundreds of times by fishing writers, "He jumped like a tarpon." No higher compliment could be paid a fish than to compare his jumps with those of a tarpon: but to keep the record straight, only a tarpon jumps like a tarpon. Louis Rhead described a leaping tarpon as "a most sinister object . . . with wide-open jaws and blood-red gills . . . as ugly a customer as one wants to meet. Its large eyes glare, its lower jaw protrudes, highly suggestive of a determined nature to smash things in general." The leap of a hooked tarpon is truly an awe-inspiring sight, not to be described by words or even photographs. By comparison, the leaps of all other fish seem feeble.

Tarpon frequently seem to bounce from one jump into the next, and the last "bounce" of a series may be as high as the first. Although I've watched many hundreds of tarpon make many thousands of jumps, I still become breathless with amazement at their remarkably speedy take-offs. There is no "get ready" or "get set" on the part of a tarpon when he decides to leap; it's just "go." Tarpon get into their jumps so rapidly that the angler sometimes finds himself wondering whether the fish doing the jumping can be the one he has on his line. This is especially apt to be the case with small tarpon weighing twenty-five pounds or less. They go into their startling leaps from any depth in the water, from dead sulks, or from sizzling runs, suddenly and unpredictably.

Because the tarpon is such a wonderful leaper, some of his other game qualities are often overlooked. Jumping isn't the only thing a tarpon does well. He is a jolting, battering fighter under the water as well as above. Few fish are more powerful; few have greater endurance; none has more courage.

Anglers are sometimes inclined to underrate the tarpon's endurance because they overlook the fact that his violent leaps demand a tremendous expenditure of energy. Few fish can muster enough vigor to make even one such leap, let alone the generous assortment offered by the tarpon. Many fish that are supposed to have great stamina simply do not fight hard enough to tire themselves out. Naturally, these fish last longer than those which give their all in desperate and furious struggle.

Some individual tarpon choose to burn their energy slowly, instead of exploding it into sky-scraping leaps. These individuals fight on and on with a plodding determination equal to or exceeding that of those marathon battlers, the jacks. I once fought a nonjumping tarpon in the twenty-pound class for three hours and twenty-five minutes with a six-ounce fly rod, and I finally lost the fish without having caused him any apparent serious fatigue. In his *Tales of Southern Rivers*, Zane Grey tells of a Panuco River tarpon weighing some two hundred pounds that towed a fisherman's skiff for well over six hours before submitting to be landed. All tarpon fishermen have experienced these extra-long fights. There is nothing exceptional about the endurance of the tarpon that wage them. Such tarpon are exceptional only in their refusal to jump away their energy.

Occasionally, however, an active, jumping tarpon puts on a real marathon. The *Miami Daily News* of June 28, 1951, carried a picture with the following caption:

"TAMPA, June 26—James VanSant of Clearwater fought this leaping 115 pound tarpon within sight of downtown Tampa traffic for 14½ hours before boating it. VanSant, fishing with Harold Lemaster, also of Clearwater, hooked the fish at 7:20 a.m. The fish jumped more than 20 times and towed their small boat around the channel all day, finally being brought to gaff at 9:50 p.m."

About a year later, in June 1952, Lemaster fought a tarpon in the same area for 18 hours, only to lose the fish when a last-ditch jump threw the hook. This fish was estimated at 130 pounds.

Don't let anyone tell you that tarpon are lacking in staying power. Remember that most tarpon fight in a sprint, while longer-lasting fish are trotters. Even the most active of tarpon display far more stamina than the average game fish, and if you ever run into a tarpon that wages a trotting fight you'll get more in the way of endurance than you'd ever wish to bargain for.

The tarpon is an enormously powerful fish, and he possesses the coordination to use his power in concentrated, explosive efforts that give him his wonderful change of pace and terrific acceleration into leaps and runs. When a hooked tarpon seems to be sulking, he is actually tensing his spring-steel muscles in preparation for his next move. With his lithe body bent in a shallow "S" shape, he'll suddenly straighten out and soar into his leap, or scream the reel as he rifles himself into a searing run. The mere straightening of his curved body or a single short sweep of his tail will suffice to project him several feet into the air or many yards through the water.

To go hand in hand with his fighting spirit and muscular coordination, the tarpon has a marvelous reserve energy, or second wind as athletes call it. Perhaps his second wind is apparent rather than actual, a manifestation of his willful determination not to give up. I'm more inclined to feel that it is attributable to his well-conditioned physique and resulting recuperative powers. At any rate, his reserve energy is amazing.

Time after time the tarpon will explode out of an apparent state of submission and into another series of wild leaps and energetic runs. Many lines and rods have been broken by "beaten" tarpon that seemed ready to be landed until the gaff was lowered. Maybe you are one of the skillful handlers of tackle who has never broken a rod on a fish. If you want to keep this fine record intact, be careful how you go about landing tarpon.

Prior to my becoming a tarpon fisherman I had never broken a rod on a fish. I had whipped an impressive assortment of pike, smallmouths, shad, big trout, stripers, channel bass, and other tough fish on light fly and casting outfits, and I had never even come close to breaking a rod. I always ridiculed the very idea of rod breakage while playing a fish; it just couldn't happen to a competent fisherman. The first time I tried fly-fishing for tarpon I broke a tip. I resolved that it would never happen again, but recently it did happen again, and it probably will happen again and again, for I certainly intend to continue the pursuit of tarpon.

The last time I broke a rod tip on a tarpon I was fly-fishing from shore in the Caloosahatchee River, catching snook and jumping an occasional baby tarpon. The fifth or sixth tarpon to grab my fly became securely hooked, and we had an exciting get-together, the fish and I. He was one of the chunky kind, about thirty inches long and weighing in the vicinity of eight pounds. After some thirty minutes of give and take, punctuated with several exhibitionistic jumps, the tarpon rolled over on his side and appeared done in. Remembering my very first experience with fly-rod tarpon (I'll never forget it), and knowing what to expect from "exhausted" silver kings, I made no attempt to land the fish, but slid him up against a rock at the water's edge. This had the desired effect of sending the fish off on a frenzied run, which ended in a pretty leap. He went down and ran again, then jumped again. I gave him the full effect of my powerful Uslan fly rod, and he broke into a series of skittering leaps. He sounded once more, but I was able to keep him moving by exerting heavy rod pressure. Ten minutes after he had first appeared whipped, the tarpon came fully four feet out of the water and landed flat on his side with a loud, crashing smack. He turned belly up, and I felt sure that he was finished. I drew him into the shore and reached for a thumb grip on his lower jaw. As I touched the fish a bucketful of water came up and hit me in the face, and I heard the sickening crack of my rod tip. Three jumps and many cusses later I landed the tarpon.

From a fish's viewpoint, the fight he wages is a good one if it gains him his freedom. A fish fights to rid himself of the hook or to break the line and make good his escape, not to please the angler or to show off in front of his schoolmates. Some individual fish may struggle valiantly and fail, and others may fight listlessly and win, but the hard fighter is more likely to ward off capture than the weak one. In a general way, the fighting ability of a fish may be evaluated by his skill at getting rid of the hook. As an escape artist, the tarpon stands unrivaled, a veritable Houdini of fishes.

There is no sure way of hooking a tarpon or keeping him hooked when using artificial lures. No matter how skilled the angler, no matter how expert the boat-handler, and no matter how free the advice of the spectators, only a small percentage of striking tarpon are landed. (If using natural bait, the fisherman may allow the tarpon—if the tarpon happens to be willing, and he frequently is not—to swallow the hook and thus sink the barb in the fish's soft, leathery gullet, but this is a cruel and unsporting way to catch tarpon and is certainly not recommended by this writer. While some guides follow the practice of trying to hook their tarpon deep, most of them instruct their clients to strike their fish while the bait is in its mouth.)

There are a number of reasons for the tarpon's success at eluding capture. In the first place, tarpon are fast strikers. They can seize, mouth, and eject an artificial lure in the twinkling of an eye, holding the lure for such a short time that the angler's strike is often too late. In the second place, tarpon have a very peculiar mouth shape. When the mouth is closed, the lower lip rests almost in line with the top of the head. When they close this mouth on a lure the impetus of the fisherman's strike doesn't carry well to the hooks. In the third place, the inside of a tarpon's mouth contains little flesh in which a hook can become firmly imbedded. The mouth is practially solid bone, with a thin, filmlike coating of gristle. In the fourth place, tarpon seem to have acutely sensitive nerves that enable them to feel the hook even before the angler feels the strike. Tarpon commonly jump and throw the hook at almost the same instant they strike it. In *The Book of the Tarpon*, A. W. Dimock mentioned this characteristic in discussing the difficulties encountered by early tarpon fishermen, stating, "Even after he had taken it [the bait] into his mouth, the touch of a hook, or the motion of a line threw him into a paroxysm of fear and the bait was cast violently from him."

These physical characteristics, coupled with his versatile and savage fighting methods, make the tarpon the most difficult of all fish to land. The landing of a tarpon, particularly on an artificial lure, gives an angler a satisfying sense of achievement, a feeling that he has accomplished a noteworthy piscatorial act. It is the feeling reserved for the conquerer of a champion, the winner of a difficult match against towering odds.

While tarpon are fish of restricted range in the United States, they are very abundant within their range. In some localities they actually seem to be increasing in numbers, rather than following the decline of most other game fish. They frequent every type of salt and brackish water within their range, and even journey far inland to spend long periods of time in fresh water. Tarpon are everybody's game fish. Neither large bank rolls, yachts, unlimited spare time, nor costly guide services are needed to find them. In South Florida they swim in every creek, river, canal, and drainage ditch that leads to salt water. Specialized tackle is unnecessary for tarpon fishing. There are tarpon of the correct size and habitat to fit any make, model, or style of rod and reel a fisherman happens to own. Majestic, wonderfully graceful, a beautiful fish in every respect, yet a rowdy roughneck at heart, the silver king tarpon is truly the greatest of game fish.

CHAPTER 3

How to Catch a Tarpon

WHEN the average fisherman thinks of tarpon, he thinks of cabin cruisers, big-game tackle, and deep waters, but to me the tarpon is a fresh-water tackle fish—the greatest light-tackle fish that ever lived. Baby tarpon are the ones I think about, frisky little two- to twenty-pounders. As a matter of fact, when the little tarpon are running in any of the creeks and canals near my home I don't think about much else. You can have your bass, or trout, or panfish; give me a fly or spinning rod, show me a little tarpon, and I'm happy.

When the tarpon is young and reckless he is a fly fish without peer. He has everything a fly-caster could want in a fish, and he has this "everything" in the superlative degree. He is smart and wary, far from being a chump or sucker for a crudely presented fly. He is capricious, and can be more exasperatingly selective than the most fastidious brown trout, then suddenly change his mood and become as enthusiastically eager as the ever willing bluegill. Happily, his mood more often than not is one of willingness to hit almost any style of fly if it is fished neatly and gently. The baby tarpon is the only fish I've ever encountered that will consistently strike an artificial fly in preference to any other bait or lure. He strikes a fly fast enough to make the strikes of all other fish seem like slow motion, so fast that you'll get the idea at times that it's impossible to hook him. And he has more game qualities than any other species of fly-hitting fish in the world!

The young tarpon is no slouch as prey for spinning and light casting tackle either. Spinning lures, especially, are almost irresistible to him at times, and spinning does have the advantage when long casts are necessary to reach the fish. Casting gear ranks a poor third for small tarpon, but when the forty- and fifty-pounders start showing up, the plug rod really comes into its own. The little five- to ten-pounders, however, seldom hit lures of plug-rod size.

I have seen baby tarpon in the ten-pound class develop bonefish complexes upon feeling the barb of a fly or spinning hook, and strip over one hundred yards of backing off the reel in less time than it takes to tell it. I have seen young tarpon jump over my boat, clearing it by several feet, then turn and jump back over it again. Again, I've met tarpon that refused to jump away their energy, investing it instead in long and gruelling underwater fights, which have sometimes lasted for as long as ten minutes per pound of tarpon flesh. This is unusual, however, for tarpon fights run to the spectacular, with double and triple jumps, and runs which can only be described as "multidirectional." The fly or spinning rod handles the tarpon's kaleidoscopic fight better than any other type of tackle—if the tarpon isn't too big!

The average tarpon is not too big for the fly or spinning rod. Although tarpon are generally thought of as big-game fish and are usually listed as averaging anywhere from forty to seventy pounds in weight, the fact is that small tarpon are much more numerous than big ones. For every tarpon of big-game size, there are scores of scrappy little chips off the old silver block. These are the baby silver kings that inhabit small rivers, creeks, and canals, and average perhaps five pounds. These are the "average" tarpon, the tarpon that can be found in South Florida in most of the waterways leading to the Gulf of Mexico at any season of the year.

Little tarpon are extremely vulnerable to artificial flies and tiny spinning lures because of their love of tidbit-sized items of food. Heavy lures can't even come close to imitating the tiny grass shrimp, skinny little minnows, and aquatic insects which make up the bulk of the baby tarpon's diet. Even big tarpon seem to like tidbit foods on occasion (I've seen barrel-chested hundred-pounders feed on minnows scarely an inch long), but baby silver kings up to ten pounds almost never feed on anything bigger than the size of minnows you'd use for crappie.

The tarpon's love of tidbits may stem from his distant relationship to the herrings. Often called a "herringlike" fish or "the largest member of the herring family," because of his appearance, the tarpon may also be called herringlike in his feeding habits. Most of the herrings prefer their food in small pieces, many of them feeding exclusively on such microscopic material as plankton. Small minnows and shrimp are to tarpon as plankton is to the herrings. Notice the shape of the tarpon's mouth. It is designed for scooping up small items of food, not for seizing large, single-course meals. I point out these facts about the tarpon's feeding habits merely to emphasize the effectiveness of small lures—flies in particular—for tarpon fishing.

I'll never forget my first experience with tarpon. I stumbled upon them while looking for bass and snook in Florida's Caloosahatchee River. They were popping, and rolling, and splashing all over the place, and I lost no time in tossing my plug right in the midst of them. They ignored it completely, not even acknowledging its existence. The tarpon looked pretty big to me, so I tried a larger plug. No dice; not even a follow. I tried every plug I had, surface, semisurface, and deep-running; but I might as well have been casting on the Sahara Desert for all the strikes I got. All this time the tarpon continued chewing up the water. I'd like to be able to say that I picked up my fly rod and caught some of those tarpon, but I didn't. It never occurred to me to try flies on them, because at that time all of my tarpon knowledge had been gleaned from books and magazines, and none of the authors I'd read had told me that flies were better than plugs for tarpon. Spinning, in those days, was practically unknown in this country.

In light of subsequent experience, I'm certain that those Caloosahatchee tarpon would have broken their necks trying to beat each other to a small streamer or spinning bucktail. I'm also certain that those tarpon were not so big as I thought, and could have been handled satisfactorily with fly tackle.

Tarpon will rise to flies of almost any sort at some time or other, but certain styles and patterns are consistently successful while others work well only on occasion. In general, saddle hackle streamers, tied either flat-wing style or with the hackles back to back to give a two-tail effect, are good. Slim bucktails, sparsely tied on 3x or 4x long shank hooks, are also good. Best surface lures are the wingless feather minnow and popping bug types, the poppers usually producing better when the water surface is ruffled, and the straight-feathered minnows being the better bet for a glassy calm. Spinners, wobbling spoons, and other items of fly-rod hardware are generally less effective for tarpon than conventional streamers or surface bugs, but there are times when the flash of a small spoon will interest fish that ignore flies. While I have taken tarpon on standard dry flies, wet flies, fly-rod plugs, and fly-and-spinner combinations, these lures are not really essential for tarpon fly-fishing.

For spinning, you can't beat weighted bucktails and streamers in the one-half- to one-eighth-ounce class. Cork-bodied bugs fished behind a bubble are also good, and there are times when the compact little metal lures of the European type work wonders. Surface plugs, such as the darters and plunkers, in one-fifth- and one-fourth-ounce sizes, occasionally produce a great deal of action, but they do not hook tarpon well. Of course, you don't have to hook tarpon to have a barrel of fun with them. Almost every strike to a surface lure will produce a spectacular jump, and tarpon fishing success is measured by the number of fish you jump rather than the poundage landed.

It is difficult to make specific color recommendations for tarpon lures because the tarpon themselves can't seem to make up their minds on this, but yellow is a must in streamers, bucktails, and surface lures. I like a bit of brown—perhaps a brown neck hackle at the head of a streamer, or some wisps of brown bucktail in the tail of a jig—in my yellow tarpon lures, but this is a personal whim, not based on any real evidence that tarpon prefer brown with their yellow. White is a good color, probably as good as yellow for streamers and bucktails. (Visibility of the fly or bucktail to the angler is very important, as baby tarpon are unbelievably fast strikers and it is necessary to watch the lure closely on the retrieve to stand much chance of hooking them.) My favorite tarpon streamer has a yellow chenille body with brown-and-yellow neck hackle and white saddle-hackle wings, tied on a size 4 hook with 4x long shank. Grizzly or Barred Rock streamers, either natural or dyed yellow, light blue, or light green, sometimes bring strikes when solid colors fail.

Blue is an amazingly effective color for tarpon at times, and every tarpon lure assortment should contain some blues. I've discovered that all-white Upperman bucktails are easily dyed blue with ordinary Rit or Tintex. These dyes work on the lacquered head as well as the hair. I would never be without a few light-blue Number 1 Uppermans when spinning for tarpon. A blue and white feather minnow is my favorite fly-rod surface lure. Tinsel-bodied bucktail streamers of yellow or white topped with black, brown, green, red, or blue make excellent tarpon flies, and they hold up better than hackle streamers. While some anglers—and good ones—swear by solid browns and blacks, I have had little success with tarpon lures that are predominantly dark in color.

For run-of-the-mill, small-water tarpon, fish of from three to ten pounds, I have found it neither necessary nor advisable to use flies or bucktails tied on hooks larger than size 1. A small hook of relatively light wire is easier to set in a tarpon's jaw than the heavy hooks so frequently used on tarpon lures. (As a matter of fact, it pays to flatten the barbs about halfway on bucktail jigs, as these lures are tied on heavy, tin-plated hooks with barbs too large for good penetration on tarpon.) The argument that small hooks will not stand up to the rigors of baby-tarpon fishing is ridiculous, for the strain exerted by a light fly or spinning outfit certainly is not sufficient to fold up any hook of respectable quality.

The fly rod for tarpon fishing may be just any rod you happen to own, or it may be a special, slow-action job especially made for use in salt water. Any good fly rod will serve OK for tarpon if you recognize its limitation. If your rod is light, do your tarpon fishing in small creeks and canals where the fish do not run large. If your rod does not have stainless steel guides, find your baby tarpon in fresh-water canals; there are as many of them in fresh water as there are in salt. Tungsten steel guides rust very rapidly in salt water, especially under the subtropical conditions where tarpon are found. Stainless steel snake guides are being supplied as standard equipment by many fly-rod manufacturers these days, so perhaps your favorite fly rod has them.

If you really want to go in for tarpon fly-fishing in particular, or salt-water fly-fishing in general, it will pay you to get a glass or plastic-impregnated bamboo rod designed for salt-water use. You'll find such a rod wonderful for bass bugging and big-stream trout fishing as well. The length and "feel" of the tarpon fly rod are matters for you to decide; you know better than anyone else what you like best. Probably the average fly-fisherman would find a bass-bug action in eight and one-half or nine feet about right.

The tarpon fly reel must be a sturdy one when used on fairly large bodies of water or when the tarpon run over five pounds. It should comfortably accommodate at least 100 yards of backing under the fly line; it must have a dependable drag; and it must be capable of withstanding the effects of salt water. It is not necessary to sink fifty or sixty dollars into the reel, however, as there are moderately priced fly reels which will serve very well. For canal fishing, where you can usually follow the hooked fish by walking along the bank, and for really little tarpon running under five pounds, just about any fly reel will do.

The reel should not be "brim-full" of line, because such overcrowding of the spool is likely to lead to the line's becoming jammed against the reel pillars when you're fighting tarpon. Tarpon must be played directly from the reel—if they're to be played successfully—and you simply can't keep up with them and see that the line is wound level at the same time. So don't stint on reel size; use one big enough to take the fly line and backing with plenty of room to spare. The best bet for serious tarpon fishing is the biggest single-action you can lay your hands on.

Most fly-fishermen have their own ideas about fly lines, and the type you like best will undoubtedly be OK with the tarpon. It is axiomatic that the line should balance with the rod, and there is no need to go into that problem here. I prefer a GAF torpedo taper in nylon, simply because I like a three-diameter line for casting, size GAF fits my rod, and nylon endures the onslaughts of salt water.

For backing, there's nothing to compare with the nylon surf and squidding lines. They are easy to splice to the fly line; their small diameter allows use of ample backing without crowding the reel spool; and their resistance to salt-water rot makes them thoroughly dependable. The backing line should be at least 100 yards long—preferably 200 for big-water fishing—and of fourteen- to twenty-five-pound test, depending on the capacity of the reel and strength of the leader. (The backing should be considerably stronger than the leader tippet, just in case a long-running tarpon decides to take it all out and break something.)

Backing line may be fastened to the fly line with either a smooth splice or a *well-trimmed* barrel knot. The splice or knot must be small enough to pass smoothly through the guides without a catch, and I know of one fisherman who learned this the hard way. I was fishing at Ortona Locks, part of the U. S. Army Corps of Engineers water-control system on the Caloosahatchee River, when this particular fellow walked up carrying a rather light fly rod strung with a heavy level line.

As he began casting, I asked, "Do you have backing under your fly line? These tarpon have been doing a lot of running today."

"Sure," he said. "A hundred yards."

After a few minutes of casting he hooked a tarpon weighing about ten pounds. The fish made a skittering jump and then broke into a sprint downriver. I heard a ripping, splintering sound followed by several paragraphs of rather strong language. When the guy stopped cussing I offered my sympathy and asked what happened.

"The damn backing knot took all the guides off my rod," he muttered.

Every guide except the stripper and tip-top had been ripped off the rod, and without guides to distribute the strain the rod had snapped at the ferrule! The fisherman had simply knotted the D level fly line to the backing, and the bulky knot was too big for the guides.

The fly leader for tarpon fishing may be any taper that straightens out well with the particular line you use, terminating in a six- to twelve-pound tippet. The lighter tippets are best for small flies, and are fine for tarpon up to four or five pounds, but leaders testing ten or twelve pounds should be used when the fish are in the five- to ten-pound class or bigger. This is because tarpon have a way of chafing leaders on their bony lips, and light tippets wear through before the larger fly-rod tarpon can be landed.

Tarpon are often decidedly line shy, and long leaders will usually produce more strikes than short ones. For best results, use leaders from seven and one-half to nine feet long. It almost goes without saying that nylon monofilament is THE material for your tarpon fly leader.

The nearest thing I've found to a perfect spinning rod for tarpon is the Sila-Flex SP65-R, with fourteen-inch handle and screw-locking reel seat. This rod has a fast tip for efficient casting of the small lures tarpon like, yet it has plenty of power in the butt for fighting your fish. While there are other good spinning rods by Conolon and Sila-Flex for tarpon fishing, the 65-R just seems to have an extra something that the others lack. At any rate, I do not feel that the big, heavy salt-water spinning rods are suitable for most tarpon fishing, as these rods simply will not cast lures in the one-eighth- to one-fourth-ounce class. Remember that your average tarpon is NOT of big-game size; he's a mere five- to ten-pounder.

The tarpon spinning reel should meet the general specifications mentioned in Chapter 1 with respect to ruggedness, drag action, line capacity and corrosion resistance. Because of the tarpon's terrific change of pace, acceleration, and speed, however, I strongly recommend using a reel with a free-running roller and full bail or manual pickup. Many times I've grooved rollers on tarpon, and I've also found that they're wizards at causing the line to wrap around finger type pickups. The Orvis reel is a fine one for small tarpon, and the Centaure with manual adapter and special stainless steel roller will handle even big silver kings well.

Six-pound-test Tynex is ample for most tarpon spinning, but it's a good idea to use a six- to eight-foot length of ten-pound test on the terminal end as a shock and abrasion absorber. This is easily tied to the casting line with a blood knot, and will not interfere with casting in any way. Use a twelve-inch leader of light Sevenstrand or Number 2 piano wire to protect your line from the tarpon's bony lips.

Your regular bass casting outfit is perfectly satisfactory for bait-casting for tarpon, but as I pointed out earlier, fly or spinning tackle will give you more action. Nevertheless, if you find tarpon in the right mood, they'll batter small surface plugs recklessly and snatch up small jigs like the three-eighth-ounce (2/0) Upperman bucktail avidly. Try fishing a jig very deep and very slowly when tarpon are around. Even when they're rolling at the surface, they seem to like their jigs deep. Don't forget the twelve-inch wire leader, or your lures won't last long when the tarpon start hitting.

I have purposely omitted any discussion of the ways and means of fishing for big tarpon, because your best bet here is to hire a guide and follow HIS—not my—instructions. Adult tarpon are very unpredictable and change their feeding habits from day to day. Then, too, the methods used success-fully at Boca Grande Pass will not work at all in the Keys, and still different tactics are necessary to catch big tarpon in the lower Caloosahatchee. For big tarpon on light fresh-water-type tackle, contact Jimmie Albright at Islamorada, Archie Cass at Miami Beach, or Bill Mann at Flamingo. In the Fort

Myers area, Eddie Fitzpatrick is a whiz at locating and hooking really big fish. For detailed information on the world's best tarpon water, Boca Grande Pass, write to Lee County Chamber of Commerce, Fort Myers, Florida. The chambers of commerce at Sarasota, Tampa, Naples and St. Petersburg can steer you right if you want to try big tarpon in any of those locales.

There are any number of places in Florida where tarpon may be taken with fresh-water tackle without even the necessity of renting a skiff. Most of the canals bordering the roads in the southern part of the state may be fished for miles on foot, with no interference except that offered by passing automobiles. Best canals for tarpon are the Tamiami Trail Canal from Ochopee to Royal Palm Hammock, the Route 84 Canal west of Fort Lauderdale, the Marco Canal below the Tamiami Trial, the Route 29 Canal on both sides of the Tamiami Trail, the Flamingo Canal below Florida City, and the Caloosahatchee Canal at Ortona Lock.

Tarpon have a preference for bends in rivers, creeks, or canals. When you're driving along an Everglades road bordered by the canal you intend to fish, give attention to every bend, for every bend is a potential tarpon hangout. Any spot where two creeks or canals meet is another probable tarpon haunt. Even the smallest ditch or most insignificant-looking feeder stream usually has tarpon around its mouth. If you can hit such a place after a shower, when water is flowing into the main creek or canal, you are bound to find tarpon. Tarpon love running water, and they feed heavily on insects and minnows washed down through ditches and small branch streams.

Other likely places for tarpon are bridges, eddies, and deep waters along mangrove-shaded shorelines. In the early morning and late evening the fish will range all over the stream, but during the hot part of the day they try to find shade.

There isn't any one infallible way to fish either fly, spinning, or casting lures for tarpon, but they do generally like a slow retrieve. Each cast should be fished to its limit, because tarpon like to be coaxed and often follow the lure for some distance before deciding to strike. The best tarpon lures, whether flies, spinning lures, or plugs, are lures with a more or less straight, darting action. Tarpon simply do not like wiggling plugs of the type used for bass in fresh water. You never can tell, though, so don't give up on tarpon before you've tried every type lure you have with every method of retrieve you can dream up. Tarpon, even young and reckless ones, are the most selective fish I know. Frequently, strikes will come to the first combination of lure and retrieve you try, but if the fish happen to be in one of their moods you'll probably have to experiment to find out what they want and how they want it. There will be times when no amount of persuading can break their stubborn disregard for your lures, and other times when you can't hit the water with anything without getting a strike. Usually, their mood will lie somewhere between these two extremes.

The tarpon is unique among fishes in that he seems to be increasing in numbers, not getting scarce as are many of our game fish. This is easily explained: having no commercial value, and being protected by Florida law, he is shunned by the netters. Anglers do not make much of a dent in his population because they lose a large percentage of their strikes and release a large percentage of their landed fish. Meanwhile, snook, sea trout, channel bass, and other fish that vie with tarpon for the available food are being reduced to such an extent that more easy meals are becoming more and more available for more and more tarpon! The concentrations of young tarpon in many South Florida waters must be seen to be believed. I repeat that neither guide, nor yacht, nor large bank roll is needed to find them. Any creek or canal leading to salt water is apt to harbor them—and South Florida is literally honeycombed with such creeks and canals! Catching a tarpon is easy. Go to it.

CHAPTER 4

The Truth About Bonefish

ONE SATURDAY morning in the summer of 1953, I set out for Key Largo for a weekend of what I hoped would be good fishing. When I left my home in Clewiston the weather seemed perfect, but during the 150-mile drive it gradually changed from good to bad to worse, with wind and rain. By the time I reached Gulfstream Fishing Lodge it was windier than three small-town politicians. Waves were breaking over the dock, and the rain merrily pitter-pattered on the windshield like shotgun pellets at close range. As I made the dash from the car to the Lodge, genial Jack Reilly cracked the door just enough to let me sift through, laughing riotously.

"What are you laughing at, you Irish soanso?" I barked.

"Sit down and have a cup of coffee," Jack laughed. "You won't get any fishing done today."

"Dammit, Jack, I drove 150 miles to fish," I said. "There must be sheltered water somewhere."

ohnny Herbert with a mixed double-header, a gag grouper and a spotted sea trout, iken on the double jig rig.

salt-water spinning, two jigs are often better than one. The :ond, or trailer, jig is easily attached by tying it on a length monofilament nylon with a snap on the other end. The snap .y then be hooked into the lower eye of the leader swivel.

His Majesty, the tarpon, greatest of Florida's many great game fish.
(*Photographed at Marine Studios.*)

Gill covers rattling like castanets, a little five-pound tarpon tries his best to shake
streamer fly he made the mistake of hitting. Small tarpon are the greatest fly

J. Nielsen shows how to release a tarpon. He is holding it upright in the water until e fish gets its breath back. The handkerchief affords a safer grip on the tarpon's wer jaw.

hese wispy and insignificant little reamers are tarpon flies—much bet- r tarpon flies, than the huge stream- s so frequently used. Tarpon have weakness for small lures.

The author with a seven-pound bonefish taken on a bucktail jig and four-pound-test line. Wading can be a very effective method of stalking bonefish.

This is the Atlantic Ocean from Upper Key Largo. Bonefish are plentiful all along these shores and may be taken by wading at any point where it's possible to reach the ocean through the dense growth of mangroves.

"Well," he said, "if you're willing to forget the reefs for a while and stoop to bonefishing, I think I can show you some sheltered water. You won't catch any bonefish on a day like this, but you can at least fish for them."

"Lead me to it," I said, gulping the last of my coffee.

"I'll take you over to Garden Cove," he said, "and you can get a skiff there. Fish the flats in the lee of the mangroves. As long as you stay close to the shore, you'll be out of the wind, and you might even catch some little 'cudas or snappers. Maybe even a bonefish, but I doubt it."

I drove the two miles to Garden Cove, following Jack Reilly's station wagon, and Jack introduced me to an old fellow who had bonefish skiffs for rent. Sure enough, there seemed to be sheltered water in the lee of the mangrove-lined shore, and the old man agreed to rent me a boat if I promised to stay in the cove. My fishing arrangements completed, Jack returned to his warm and dry lodge, pausing just long enough to make an uncalled-for remark about the eccentric customers he had to please.

I lost no time in loading the skiff and getting out on the sheltered flat. It became apparent immediately that the flat was not so sheltered as it appeared from the dock, as the wind seemed to hedge-hop over the mangroves and skim just above the water. My efforts with the pole were not particularly effective, but the tide was high enough to accommodate operation of my ten-horse outboard. Although an unconventional if not heretic piece of bonefish-stalking equipment, the motor worked fine, allowing me to idle along the edge of the mangroves while casting blind out over the flat.

I had covered perhaps fifty yards when I felt something take the little bucktail. After a momentary pause to give the fish time to turn, I hit him hard. Skittering across the water came a six-inch barracuda. "Well, I'm not skunked, anyway," I laughed.

Soon I got a bigger 'cuda, then another, and while I was fighting the second one I saw the beckoning flash of a bonefish tail! He was a good hundred yards away, and well out from the mangroves. Horsing the barracuda in, I yanked the motor into life and literally roared in the direction of that bonefish. Suddenly realizing that I was operating in two feet of water, I cut the throttle and let the boat drift. Then I saw him, a dark shadow vaguely defined under the rain-spattered surface of the water. He was less than fifty feet away, and the wind was drifting me down on him at what seemed a fantastic rate. I slung a snap cast in the general direction of the bonefish, but the wind caught the line and arched the bucktail some twenty-five or thirty feet behind him. I began to reel like mad to try to get in another cast, but the bonefish was too fast for me. He spun about and rushed the lure, catching it before I realized what happened. Automatically I set the hook, and the bonefish headed for the open sea.

By this time, my skiff had drifted out into the full force of the wind and was skidding across the water fast. The bone-fish was quartering into the wind, and the opposing directions of the drifting boat and running fish fairly melted the line off my reel. I had plenty of line, some 500 or 600 yards, but if a bonefish gets as much as 150 or 200 yards of six-pound or lighter line on a shallow, grass-bottomed flat, the cause is as good as lost. As soon as he starts to circle, the line hangs in the grass and goes to pieces. There was only one thing to do, and that was to grab for the starting cord on the motor. The ever reliable Johnson responded instantly to my awkward, backhanded pull, and in no time at all I had things under control. Keeping the skiff within a hundred yards of the fish, I took no chances and played him lightly until he meekly submitted to the net.

As I hoisted him aboard I noticed that he seemed to pack a bit more than average weight. "Maybe I'd better keep him" I thought. "He might make a *Field & Stream* entry." The longer I looked at him, the bigger the bonefish grew, so I decided to quit while I was ahead and weigh him in. Besides, I was beginning to waterlog badly, and I knew there was hot coffee back at the lodge.

Jack Reilly was still laughing when he met me at the door. "Back already?" he asked. "I thought you liked to fish."

I held up the bonefish. "Where are your scales?" I demanded.

Jack stared at the fish and shook his head. "You are without doubt the luckiest bonefisherman I've ever seen."

The scales said eight pounds ten ounces, and darned if that bonefish didn't win out in the spinning division of the 1953 *Field & Stream* contest!

Unfortunately, most of the stories and book chapters published about bonefish have attempted to create the impression that only the most highly skilled fisherman has any business fooling with them. The truth of the matter is that the angler of average skill and experience should have no trouble catching bonefish if he goes about it right. Rather than trying to convince you that you can't catch a bonefish, I'm going to tell you how you can. While it may not be the easiest fishing you ever tried, who wants easy fishing? You can be sure of one thing: it will be the most habit-forming fishing you've ever run across.

The bonefish is one of the "herringlike" fishes, related to the ladyfish and the tarpon. There is little danger of confusing the bonefish with his relatives, however, for he looks different, behaves differently, and has entirely different feeding habits. Strictly a shallow-water feeder, the bonefish uses deep water only for traveling, loafing out a tide, or keeping cool when the waters of shallow flats get too hot for comfort. While bonefish are occasionally caught from water of greater depth than three feet, such catches must be considered accidental. If you want to be reasonably certain of catching bonefish, you must go after them on the flats. In the tropical and subtropical regions where bonefish are found, the water is so clear you can sometimes count the pebbles under fifty feet of it. It goes without saying, then, that you're going to have to use a careful approach to do business with fish feeding in a mere foot or two of water like this. Small wonder the bonefish has acquired such a reputation for wariness and timidity!

I haven't found that bonefish are particularly hard to fool—even with artificial lures. Certainly they are no tougher than most other fish in clear water. As in the case of other fish, it's easier to fool the small ones than the big ones, but even big bonefish are pretty careless about what they take internally at times.

The bonefish does his feeding by cruising over the flats against the tide, grubbing in the mud, pausing now and then to take things into his mouth, and spitting them out again when their taste doesn't suit him. It is this habit of sampling interesting-looking objects that makes the bonefish highly vulnerable to artificial lures.

The general notion is that bonefish feed only on the rising tide, but this is erroneous. There are flats suitable for low-tide feeding, half-tide feeding, and high-tide feeding, and bonefish use them accordingly. As a general rule, bonefish work in water from eight inches to two and one-half feet in depth, and they don't care which way the tide is going if the water depth and food supply meet with their approval.

Hard-fighting fishes are generally gluttonous feeders and smashing strikers. Not the prissy bonefish. He feeds daintily, nosing around through the grass, poking his snout into crab holes, turning over shells to root out and sample interesting bits of commissariat. Under no circumstances does the bonefish bolt his food or snatch it greedily. He is even polite to his schoolmates, not subscribing to the every-fish-for-himself attitude adopted by most fish at mealtime. Such prim social and table manners serve by comparison to magnify greatly the first run for freedom he makes when hooked—although the run IS a good one; probably the best of any inshore fish.

I like to find bonefish in extremely thin water late in the evening when the surface is slick. Under these conditions you can see the wakes of cruising fish a long distance off, and tails stand out boldly. Then, when you cast ahead of and beyond a bonefish and watch his wake close in on your lure, wondering whether he'll take it or pass it up, the suspense is so electric you can hardly stand it. Suddenly the wake ends in a swirl, you feel a weight, and he's on. This is one of the greatest thrills the sport of fishing has to offer.

Bonefish are extremely curious, and it is frequently possible to take advantage of their curiosity to catch them. They will often follow your boat as it drifts or is poled across the flat, sometimes even circling after flushing from the boat to come up behind for a look at the thing that scared them. It pays, then, to give plenty of attention to the water behind you, whether you're wading, drifting or poling.

Captain Jack Reilly, of Reilly's Beachhead on Upper Key Largo, has guided bonefishermen for many years, and he has had some funny experiences with bonefish. On one occasion, Jack was poling a guy over a flat en route to a good spot for still-fishing. They carried a mesh bag containing live shrimp over the side of the boat, standard practice when using a bonefish skiff with no bait well. Jack's client happened to glance down at the bag of shrimp, and there was a bonefish trying to pull a shrimp through the mesh! This while the skiff was being poled along in only two feet of water! Since that experience, Jack has kept an eye on the shrimp bag and has seen bonefish attracted to it many times.

Bonefish have an unbelievably acute sense of smell, and when they're hungry the odor of food makes them lose practically all of the caution for which they are noted. This, of course, makes them very susceptible to chumming, and it's pretty safe to say that if bonefish won't come to chum they aren't apt to hit anyway. Best chum is a smashed conch shell (with the conch inside), but pieces of shrimp, crab, or other shellfish will work well too. A smashed live conch is superior to pieces of conch flesh for chum because the bonefish cannot get at the meat after being attracted by its aroma. Their resulting frustration renders them suckers for your lure or bait!

Far and away the most suitable and effective tackle for bonefishing is spinning gear. An experienced spin-caster can take bonefish consistently when all other fishing methods fail. The fly rod can be deadly on bonefish too, but it takes a good fly-caster to achieve consistent results. The very breeze that keeps the Florida Keys comfortably cool even in summer is generally strong enough to make the average fly-caster hot under the collar. Bait-casting for bonefish is a highly specialized trick; feasible, but not practical for any but the well-seasoned bonefisherman. The classic bonefishing gear consists of a six and one-half-foot rod with light tip and a 1/0 reel full of six-thread (eighteen-pound) linen or the equivalent in nylon line. This is used for still-fishing, with a light sinker, a couple of 2/0 or 3/0 snelled hooks, and baits of shrimp, hermit crab, finny crab or conch.

I mentioned earlier that bonefish have a weakness for tasting interesting-looking objects to see if they're edible. Show them an interesting lure, one small enough for them to mouth easily, and there's an excellent chance that they'll try it. Therein lies the effectiveness of spinning tackle. The small lures fit readily into the bonefish's small mouth, they can be cast accurately and quietly, and the nearly invisible mono-filament line doesn't arouse the bonefish's suspicious nature. On a recent trip to Key Largo I hooked seven successive bonefish on a size 1 Upperman bucktail before spotting a fish that refused to strike. By way of comparison, four other fishermen still-fishing on the same flat at the same time did not get a single strike on live shrimp. At dinner that night the unsuccessful anglers told me that plenty of bonefish nosed around their baits, but just wouldn't pick them up. Why, they wanted to know, did the fish strike a bit of lead and bucktail, yet refuse live shrimp?

Frankly, I don't know why, but I have a few theories. For one thing, perhaps the bonefish weren't in the mood for shrimp. They KNEW they didn't want shrimp, but a buck-tail—well, maybe they just wanted to try the taste of it. Then, there was the light monofilament line I used. The still-fishermen were using standard six-thread cuttyhunk, which looks like tow-rope in the ultraclear water of a Keys flat. It is possible that the bonefish would have taken shrimp fished on monofilament nylon.

In any event, spinning tackle and small bucktails are the most killing combination I know for bonefish. Spinning bucktails won't get all of the bonefish all of the time, but if fished properly they'll come closer to it than any other bait or lure. The proper way to fish a bucktail depends on whether you're spotting your fish first and stalking them, or casting blind.

When you sight a bonefish and work to within casting range of him, try to "lead" him with your cast so that the lure passes just in front of him. This means casting at least six feet beyond the fish, so that the splash of the lure doesn't startle him, and far enough in front of him so that his speed of travel doesn't take him past the lure before you can retrieve it through his line of vision. This is a great deal easier than it sounds—unless the sight of a bonefish gives you buck fever. The retrieve should be erratic, and just fast enough to keep the bucktail out of the grass on bottom. Of course, you can speed your retrieve when necessary to bring the bucktail in front of a rapidly moving bonefish, slowing it down as it comes into his line of vision. If a bonefish should follow the bucktail for some distance, changing the speed of your retrieve may produce an immediate strike.

I like yellow or white bucktails for bonefish, for the simple but very important reason that I can see them well in the water. Even in blind-casting, it helps to be able to see your lure, for if you watch it closely during the retrieve you may frequently see a shadow following it. This, of course, calls for a change in retrieve speed.

Blind-casting is not the best way to catch bonefish, but under some conditions it's the only way. When the water is much over two feet deep, the wind is strong, or clouds obscure the sun, bonefish can be mighty hard to see, and if you try to spot a fish before making a cast you may not even get your line wet. The best way to cast blind is to allow your boat to drift with the wind, casting ahead of it and off to the side, with an occasional shot behind the boat for the curious bonefish that may be following. The retrieve for this kind of fishing must be gauged to allow for the speed of the drifting boat; faster when you're drifting toward your lure, and slower when drifting away from it. Blind-casting a wind-swept flat is a cinch with spinning tackle, and it's surprisingly productive.

Recently I was blind-casting from a drifting skiff right in front of Jack Reilly's dock, using spinning tackle and a size 1 Upperman bucktail. The wind was a battering thirty-mile gale, small craft warnings were up, and there I was again trying to fish a bonefish flat! Anyway, one of my retrieves was stopped suddenly by a solid tug, and a fish was on. For quite a while I couldn't figure out what sort of fish it was, as it tugged like a grouper or jack and just plodded about instead of running fast like a bonefish. Finally it did decide to run, however, and I had to crank up my outboard and follow. Then around, and around, and around the boat the fish swam, first on a hundred-yard radius and then in ever diminishing circles, until I gradually pumped him to within reach of my landing net. It was a bonefish, and a good one, a bonefish that fought himself out so completely I could not revive him to set him free. He weighed just under eight pounds.

Fly-fishing for bonefish differs from spinning only in the mechanics of the method. The slow, erratic retrieve; placement of the fly in front of and beyond the fish; and the change of retrieve speed to get the followers—all constitute good technique with flies as well as with spinning gear. It is not so easy, however, to snap out a fly-cast to intercept a cruising bonefish as it is with spinning tackle. Best flies are small bucktail or hackle streamers, about size 1 or 1/0, predominantly white or yellow in color for good visibility. Blind-casting for bonefish with fly tackle is an arm-breaking task, and is not recommended as a general fishing method.

The principal requirements for either fly or spinning tackle for bonefishing are quality and line capacity. The reel, especially, absorbs a terrific going over, and it doesn't take many bonefish to unwrap a poorly made one. The spinning reel should have a capacity for 200 yards of six-pound line; it must have a metal—not plastic—spool, a stainless, smooth-running roller, and corrosion resistance throughout. Plastic spools, nylon excepted, will often split under the pressure exerted by the line during a bonefish run. If the roller doesn't turn freely, the monofilament line will melt under the heat it generates. And since corrosion will cause any reel to operate at below maximum smoothness, no corrosion can be tolerated in a reel for bonefishing. Probably the best bet for bonefish spinning is a high-grade salt-water spinning reel, but there are fresh-water-size reels, too, that serve very well. For fly-fishing, use a BIG single-action reel, with chrome line guard and a dependable, adjustable drag. Most fly reels big enough to hold your fly line and 200 yards of eighteen-pound-test nylon backing will meet the other requirements.

With certain qualifications, the exact style of spinning or fly rod for bonefishing is largely a matter of personal preference. It goes without saying that all the hardware must be immune to salt-water corrosion. The length of the rod, whether fly or spinning, is for you to decide; but remember that the longer the rod, the higher you can hold the line when a bonefish is sweeping over a flat with it. A high-held rod will save many a fish that might otherwise be lost on coral, sea fans, or grass. I like a seven-foot spinning rod with a slightly stiff action for bonefish, and for fly-casting, a nine-footer on the slow side. A metal reel seat is to be preferred over reel bands for the spinning rod, but is not absolutely essential if the bands fit well. As far as I'm concerned, there's only one material for salt-water fishing rods any more, and that one material is hollow glass.

Six-pound-test Tynex monofilament nylon makes the best all-around line for most bonefish flats, but it pays to carry an extra spool of eight-pound line to use when floating grass is abundant or sea fans grow nearby. I often use a six-foot length of eight-pound monofilament tied by a blood knot to the terminal end of my six-pound line, to take the wear and tear of being dragged along the bottom by bonefish as they try to scrape the hook loose.

The most foolproof way of catching a bonefish is to hire an experienced guide to show you the ropes. He'll pole you across the flats, spot the fish for you, and work the boat to within casting range, so that all you have to do is make your cast. A good guide knows just where to find bonefish at any particular stage of the tide, time of day, or season, and this alone eliminates most of the uncertainty. If you're on your toes, you can learn enough on one guided bonefishing trip to do pretty well on your own next time out.

Guides are not essential to bonefishing success, although many of them like to make you think they are. You can rent a skiff at any number of places in the Florida Keys, consult the boat liveryman about the location of the nearest bonefish flat, and go get 'em. Maybe you'll have ideal conditions, with the wind blowing away from the sun and with the tide, so that you can drift with the sun at your back as you keep watch ahead of the skiff for bonefish. When the sun's at your back it is shining into the eyes of any bonefish that happen to be facing you, and you can get very close before they see you. Maybe you won't have perfect conditions, but you can still catch bonefish. If the wind drifts you into the sun, try to spot your fish off to the side rather than directly ahead of the boat. After all, there is no reason why all the bonefish should be in your direct line of drift. Try to look *through* the water instead of *at* it, focusing your eyes on the bottom. Polaroid glasses and a little practice will make this easier than it sounds. When drifting a flat, don't hesitate to throw a cast at anything that looks even remotely like a fish. Cast first, and wonder what it was you cast to later. The casts you make to dark clumps of grass, rocks, and shadows don't cost you a thing—and you'd be surprised how many "shadows" turn out to be bonefish. If your visibility is so limited as to make sighting fish unlikely, cast blind. You'll get enough action from barracuda to hold your interest, and every now and then you'll latch onto a bonefish.

Hooking and playing bonefish is not particularly difficult, so long as you keep your head. As a rule they strike slowly, and there is greater danger of missing them by striking back too soon than too late. When using an artificial lure, delay your strike until you are sure the bonefish has it in his mouth, or better still, wait until you feel him. In thin water the impulse to strike too soon is almost overpowering when a bone-

fish wake plows the water around the lure. Wait! Play bonefish with a light drag, for they'll run just as far against a heavy
one, with a greater chance of breaking the line or leader in
the grass. Hold your rod as high as you can get it until the
long first run has ended, then pump the fish back. If you can
get him back after his first run, he's your fish, as the succeeding
runs are short and relatively slow. Unhook him gently, hold
him upright in the water until he regains his breath and
balance, and release him. A dead bonefish is worthless.

Bonefish are found in varying degrees of abundance from
Miami south to Key West. Key Largo seems to harbor the
greatest concentration, and their average size, too, is greatest
here. At this writing, the bonefish I've caught on Key Largo
have averaged over six pounds—says the De-Liar—and I have
never caught a bonefish smaller than four pounds in this area.

There is no definite "best" season for bonefish, but spring
and fall might have a slight edge over the rest of the year. The
slowest season is the hot, calm period of "dog days" in July
and August, but even then you can have some fine bonefishing
in the cool of the morning or late evening.

For the sheer beauty and charm of it, bonefishing is just
about as pleasant a pastime as you'll ever run across. It is intensely fascinating just to drift over the sparkling waters of a
Florida Keys flat and allow your imagination to revel in what
your eyes see: a shark's pulsating dorsal fin in the distance, the
darting flight of an awesome Florida lobster, the cold stare of
a fearless young barracuda, the formal symmetry of sea urchins
amidst waving ribbon grass on the white bottom, the kaleidoscopic flashes of multitudes of tiny tropical fishes.

So you want to catch a bonefish? Go to it! And if you can
use a partner, look me up, and I'll go with you.

CHAPTER **5**

Snook Are Big for Their Size

I'LL NEVER forget the day we introduced Floyd Dobbins to snook fishing. Floyd was a dyed-in-the-wool bass fisherman and a pretty good one, at that. Bass men are notoriously hard to convince when you try to impress them with the merits of other fish.

In the car en route to Ortona Locks on the Caloosahatchee River, C. J. Nielsen and I briefed Floyd on the coarser points of angling for *Centropomus undecimalis*. We raved so enthusiastically about the snook's savage game qualities that Floyd soon discounted everything we had told him as exaggerated build-up. C. J. and I exchanged knowing grins and said no more. Snook can speak for themselves.

When we had pulled into our parking spot at Ortona, I suggested that Floyd try a small, yellow, rubber-skirted, deep-running plug; and instructed him to fish it parallel to the rocky shore. He wanted to know what to do if a snook should strike, but I assured him that an old experienced bass man like himself would have no trouble. After all, he knew how to handle big bass, didn't he?

When Floyd finally began casting, I left him and headed for a favorite location of mine a couple of hundred yards upstream. I hadn't walked fifty steps when the fun began.

Floyd's voice could have been heard a half-mile away. "I got 'im!" he screamed.

I spun around just in time to see an average-size snook explode into the air and send Floyd's plug crashing into the rocks twenty feet above the waterline.

"You *had* 'im!" C. J. cracked.

"Oh, damn! Oh, damn! Oh, damn! What a fish!" wailed Floyd. "What a fish!"

"If you think that little five-pounder was a fish, we'll be in for quite a show if you hang a good one," needled C. J.

"You saw 'im, Phil," Floyd pleaded. "He went ten pounds easy, didn't he?"

"Frankly, Floyd, I doubt that he even went five," I truthfully replied.

"Biggest five-pound fish *I* ever saw," muttered Floyd.

Floyd long ago became a confirmed snook angler, and will probably admit that the first snook he hung was not even a five-pounder; but he'll still insist that it was the biggest five-pound fish he ever saw. Snook have a way of looking big on the end of a line. I suspect the illusion is due to a combination of factors: the broad fin span, the large mouth, the long head, the wide-spreading gill-covers, and the very high pulling-power-per-pound ratio. The jolting strike and savage initial rush of a four- or five-pound snook spells "BIG FISH" to every tyro at the snook fishing game. Don't be too disappointed when your first "big" snook fails to weigh as much as you expected. Snook do not merely look big and feel big; they *are* big—for their size.

A couple of years ago I was fishing from shore below Ortona Locks when a stranger sporting a Midwestern accent approached and asked what kind of fish I was after.

"Snook," I said. "This is a good spot for them."

"Snook? What in the world's a snook?"

I gave him a brief discourse on the excellent game qualities of snook, discussing their habits and mentioning a few of the best ways to catch them. "Snook are mighty rugged fish," I concluded. "There's something about them that no other fish can duplicate."

With a skeptical smile, my new acquaintance said, "I'm from Wisconsin, and I've caught lots of muskies. Your snook would have to go some to beat them."

"Well," I said, "the snook aren't hitting now, but you never can tell when they'll start. If you've got some tackle in your car, maybe you can catch one for comparison."

The gent from Wisconsin thought this a good idea, and walking up to his car, he dug out a heavy casting outfit and tackle box. His rod was a top-grade four and one-half-foot solid steel job, and his reel, too, was a good one, full of thirty-pound-test line. A more or less regulation musky outfit. I gave him a wire leader, and poked through his tackle box to find a red and white Pikie, suggesting that he fish it with a whipping motion for best results.

I watched him cast for a few minutes, and, satisfied that he was doing a good snook-fishing job, returned to my own casting. Suddenly I heard a grunt and the clacking of a reel handle on knuckles. Out of the water surged a fighting mad snook of about fifteen pounds, shaking with mouth open, gill covers distended, and fins spread wide as only a snook can spread them. Wisconsin had connected, but the sight of that snook was too much for him, and he froze to the reel handle in an acute attack of buck—or snook—fever. The heavy line cracked like a whip as it parted.

"That, my friend, was a snook," I informed my dazed companion. "How did he compare with your muskies?"

He slowly shook his head. "You're right, there's something about a snook," he conceded.

There's something about a snook—especially a big snook —that causes even the experienced fisherman to forget all he knows about playing fish. Rare is the angler who can take his first big snook in stride, no matter how many big fish of other species he's caught. Snook affect different fishermen in different ways, but the most common reaction they cause is that of freezing up on the reel. I have often seen skilled rod-handlers play big snook beautifully until the first jump, then freeze up and break the line. Indeed, this reaction is so common that fishermen who habitually use the lightest of tackle for everything from Gulf Stream trolling to tarpon fishing stick to service reels and forty-pound line when bait-casting for snook. They know they're going to freeze up in spite of themselves.

A less frequent form of snookitis exhibits the symptom of extreme, almost ridiculous caution in playing snook. This is the type that afflicts me. Normally I play fish hard, even with light gear, and land them in pretty good time. When I hang a big snook, however, I just can't work up the courage to pour it on. This is almost as bad as freezing up, because snook will nearly always work the hooks out if you give them enough time. A few years ago I babied a huge snook for forty-five minutes, using practically no thumb pressure during his runs, and leading him very gently each time he turned my way. When finally exhausted, the four-foot monster turned belly up in the middle of the river, about thirty yards out, and the plug dropped out his mouth. The fish was so tired that the current carried him several yards before he righted himself and slowly swam away.

Just why snook affect fishermen the way they do I can't say, but I can tell you right here and now that the snook is a fighting fish. He's a fighting fish from the tip of his pugnacious lower jaw to the tip of his broad tail, on the hook or off, a slugger who neither asks nor gives quarter to fishermen or other fish. A fish of many moods, sometimes irritable and belligerent, sometimes congenial, and sometimes coldly aloof, the snook belongs on anybody's list of top ten American game fish.

Battling with a boisterous enthusiasm that few other fish can match, the snook gives the impression that he actually enjoys fighting a hook and line. He doesn't just fight; he brawls, using rough-and-tumble tactics combined with clever maneuvers fair and foul. He'll run, and jump, and throw his weight around with the best of 'em, and if this fails, he'll not hesitate to hit below the belt. Yes, sir, the snook is a fighting fish.

Snook are relatively slender fish, shaped more or less like a walleye. The head is decidedly pikelike, being long and flattened, with the lower jaw protruding in a pugnacious manner. The color is silvery, varying from the light, ghostly silver of the surf-dwelling snook to the tarnished-appearing silver of the creek and river fish. The lateral line is invariably as black as the proverbial ace of spades.

Like most American game fish, the snook is well fixed for local names. Robalo, sargent fish, brouchet de mer (meaning sea pike), and ravallia are a few of the more common ones. The name snook incidentally is pronounced "snuke" by Floridians. While I prefer to rhyme the snook with hook, I do not intend to make an issue of it. If Floridians invented the name, they have a perfect right to invent the pronunciation.

Loosely speaking, the snook may be defined as any member of the genus *Centropomus*. There are known to be three species of snook in Florida waters, another in the West Indies, and at least two in the Pacific south of the continental United States. Of the three Florida snooks, one is a runty little fellow scarcely a foot long. This fish is rare and is of no interest to the fisherman. Another of the Florida snooks is fairly plentiful on the lower east coast, reaching a top weight of about four pounds. The "common" snook is the big, rawboned *Centropomus undecimalis*. He averages three or four pounds in weight and grows to sixty. Ten-pounders are very common, and a number weighing over thirty pounds are taken in Florida each year. When a fisherman speaks of snook, this is the one he has in mind.

Ranging from the northern coast of South America through the Caribbean islands, along the shores of the Gulf of Mexico, and over the southern half of Florida's east coast, the snook may be classified as an inshore, tropical and sub-tropical salt-water species. He never ventures very far from shore, preferring to swim along the beaches and among the roots of the mangrove trees, which comprise the shore line of the greater part of his range. He loves to ascend creeks and rivers into fresh water, and indeed shows many characteristics of a fresh-water fish. Dr. Luis R. Rivas of the University of

Miami Marine Laboratory (who is probably the world's top authority on snook) states that any given snook will spend about half his lifetime in fresh water. Where the food supply is adequate, some individuals never leave the fresh-water creek or canal in which they were hatched, while others develop wanderlust and seek their fortunes in the salt.

Bill Johnson, who operates a fishing camp at Clewiston on Lake Okeechobee, told me one of my favorite snook stories. It seems he rented a boat and outboard motor to a couple of ardent bass-fishing tourists. He gave them instructions as to where they'd be sure to find bass, then forgot them for a while. In a couple of hours the bass boys were back. Their speech was incoherent, but their babbling seemed to indicate that they had run into a school of the world's largest bass. All their plugs were gone, little line remained on their reels, and their nerves were shattered. Patient questioning gave Bill the answer: They had become involved with a school of snook.

It is not unusual to find snook as far inland as Lake Okeechobee. They are great wanderers, and during high-water periods they show up in all sorts of places where you wouldn't expect to find them. It is quite likely that many snook use the cross-Florida waterway to travel between the Gulf of Mexico and the Atlantic Ocean. Some of the finest snook fishing I've experienced has occurred more than forty miles inland.

There has been an effort by Florida sportsmen during the last few years to have the snook declared a fresh-water fish for purposes of sparing them from commercial fishing, but so far the efforts have met with failure. The commercial snook toll remains appallingly heavy, and it is about time tourist-minded Florida woke up to the tourist value of this great gamester. Snook are still plentiful enough to lure many Northern fishermen back again and again to Florida, and I know of at least one man who moved his manufacturing business down from New York so that he could fish for snook every day. Inshore fish like the snook are extremely vulnerable to stop nets, haul seines, and other such cruelly efficient devices, and unrestricted commercial fishing CAN eliminate the snook completely . . . or at least make him a rare fish. The snook isn't rare yet, however, and he never will be if all snook fans take up the cry on his behalf.

Among salt-water bait-casters in southern Florida the snook is easily the most popular fish, for he is the best all-round casting-rod fish you'll ever encounter anywhere. Picture a fish with the quick temper of the largemouth bass, the speed of the pike, and the contrariness of the muskie, along with the power and stamina developed in the intensely competitive struggle for survival in salt water. Imagine a fish like that, lurking under shore-line cover, just waiting for a plug to land right next to the bank, waiting for a chance to wallop the paint off it, or maybe to ignore it . . . but waiting. A bait-caster's dream fish, that's the snook.

Snook may be ridiculously easy to fool (actually, I don't think they are really fooled; they just don't give a hoot) or they may be totally indifferent to any lure you show them. These extremes are met with regularly by snook fishermen, but there's not much you can do about snook when you find them in either mood—except catch 'em or cuss 'em, as the case dictates. Generally, however, snook are just hard enough to catch to be interesting, and just easy enough to hold the attention of the impatient fisherman. Snook tend to be very lure conscious and particular about details of style, size, and action of the lure. Experienced snook fishermen know this, but newcomers to the game seem to be slow in catching on. Keep this fact in mind while we discuss the better snook lures and the ways to fish 'em.

Probably the most consistent snook lures for both the plug and spinning rods are the feather, bucktail and nylon jigs. It's a safe bet that more snook are taken on jigs than on all other artificial lures combined. Jigs are especially effective in inlets and passes, in the surf, and in any water deeper than five or six feet. Jigs do an excellent job when the snook are lying right on bottom, for they can be cast uptide and allowed to sink into pay dirt. The retrieve for this fishing should be slow and whippy, executed so that the lure jumps sharply off the bottom, then plunges down again, kicking up a cloud of sand. Should several such retrieves over a given spot fail to produce, try reeling like mad after two or three bounces. If this tactic proves unsuccessful, remember that snook are particular, and don't give up yet. Try a slow, steady retrieve, dragging the jig along the bottom. These are the three best ways to work a jig for snook, but they're not the only ways. Don't hestitate to experiment with any ideas you have before throwing in the sponge.

Color, insofar as I have been able to determine, is of little importance in a jig for snook, but there are plenty of darn good snook fishermen who claim otherwise. Yellow is certainly the most popular hue, with red and white a poor second. You can't go wrong with either color.

Underwater plugs, both the floating and diving and the slow sinkers, are often necessary in snook fishing. The slow sinkers like the standard River Runt sometimes perform snook-catching miracles in deep water during the winter months. I used to think that most of the snook deserted the upper

Caloosahatchee River in January and February, because the old reliable lures and methods took very few snook during these months. Then one New Year's Day I stumbled onto a method that has since paid big dividends in midwinter snook fishing. In experimenting with different lures I snapped on a River Runt sinker, flipped a cast to the middle of the river, and allowed the plug to sink for five seconds before retrieving. The next cast was allowed seven seconds of sinking time, and I had barely started the retrieve when a snook latched on. More experimentation proved that the count was very important, indicating that the snook were lying at a particular midwater level and that they would not venture far from that level to pursue the plug. Strangely enough, the proper sinking time for any given plug at any given spot in the river seemed to remain constant, not only for one day, but for every winter since! That much I'll tell you, but the location of the five-, seven- and ten-second spots you'll have to discover for yourself.

Color in underwater plugs seems to make considerable difference to snook. Yellow is good, as are blue scale, red and white, and yellow perch. When in doubt, use yellow.

For the most fun with snook, either casting or spinning, there's nothing like top water plugs. No other fish of comparable size wallops a surface lure like a snook. And when they are in shallow water, no other lure excites them like a surface lure.

While nearly all types of surface lures will take snook from time to time, the best by far are the darters and zaragossas. Plunkers and poppers are good, but plugs that can be pulled beneath the surface during the retrieve are preferred by most snook addicts, for a reason described later.

Snook demand action, and lots of it, in a top water lure, action that can be imparted only by the rod. The retrieve proper should be at no more than moderate speed, but the lure should dive, and dart, and jump very rapidly. This can be accomplished with a high-held rod with fast tip action. Work the rod with a short, fast whipping motion, reeling all the while to keep the line in front of the lure so the hooks won't foul it. This retrieve is very difficult to describe, but it's not too hard to execute after you get the feel of it. It will take snook when everything else fails.

Work shore lines for snook just the way you'd work them for bass—except for the retrieve. Cast the plug well up under the mangroves and bring it out jumping. If a fish swirls behind the lure repeatedly without striking, make a long sweep of the rod to pull the plug under—and be prepared for a jolt! Surface lures worked conventionally will catch snook, too, so if it takes a while to master the "snook" retrieve don't be discouraged.

I don't believe that its color has a great deal to do with the success or failure of a surface lure for snook. Yellow, silver flash, or red and white are as good as any. Size of the lure, however, is very important. If snook show interest in, say, a five-eighths-ounce darter, yet refuse to hit it, try a three-eighths-ounce size. Incidentally, the little one-fifth- and one-fourth-ounce spinning darters and injured minnows are the most consistent topwater snook lures I've ever tried. They, too, work best when retrieved dancing *à la* St. Vitus.

While snook up to four or five pounds are active and spectacular fighters when taken on a fly, the big ones hardly realize they're hooked, and their fight is slow and drawn out.

Big snook can be taken with fly tackle, true, but a casting outfit is more practical and better suited for the job.

Granting that the fly rod may be inferior to either the casting or spinning outfit as a snook weapon on a total-poundage basis under a long-term trial, it cannot be denied that flies are amazingly effective at times. Though voracious, snook can be exasperatingly selective—particularly when they're feeding on small minnows. During these periods of selectivity, small streamer flies often work wonders.

Snook in the one- to five-pound class are great fly fish, with a special weakness for slim streamers and bucktails. Flies are especially good in small waters where the splash of larger lures seems to put the fish down. In canals like the one along the Tamiami Trial between Ochopee and Royal Palm Hammock, streamers and surface bugs will take snook at a ten to one rate over casting lures, and probably two to one over spinning lures. Repeated presentation of the fly to all likely looking spots is the key to productive snook fishing via the fly rod. A snook can turn up his nose at a streamer for just so long, then his will power breaks down and he gobbles it. Streamers and bucktails about three inches long, tied on hook sizes for 2 to 1/0, are about right for snook. Combinations of yellow, white, and blue will cover the color requirements.

One morning in summer, my wife and I stopped by a man-grove-lined creek on the road to Fort Myers Beach. Our objective was fly-rod tarpon. Although no tarpon were rolling, we decided to try a few casts anyway. Noticing a slight disturbance under the branches of a mangrove, I dropped the streamer near the spot. The response was instantaneous. A fish hit before I had even started the retrieve, and in a few minutes I had the pleasure of releasing a two-pound snook. Doris also hooked one on her first cast, but he managed to snip her leader with his gill blades. The rapid activity soon had several cars stopped and several anglers casting plugs, spoons, and feather jigs. For Doris and me, with our little size 6 green-and-white bucktails, it was a strike on every cast; but for the casting-rod bunch, it was a complete skunking. We landed and released fourteen snook ranging from two to four pounds before the action tapered off. Had we been equipped with casting outfits only, we'd have drawn a blank! On that same day we caught snook on flies at every creek along the road, yet every bait-caster we met had been unable to raise a fish.

Why should every snook in every creek within a radius of ten miles decide to feed on small stuff at the same time? Don't ask me, brother! All I can tell you is that they do it regularly.

Small poppers and feather minnows often prove better than streamers for snook in canal fishing. These lures are at their best when the snook are feeding selectively on small minnows or grass shrimp, probably because they float high and the fish can't see them well. Last fall I drove down to the Tamiami Trail and found the snook popping inch-long minnows all over the canal. I started first with spinning tackle, but after thirty minutes of casting with several different lures I hadn't even had a strike. Next I tried the fly rod, using a small streamer, and although I managed to cast it almost into the mouths of feeding snook, this too drew a blank. The last resort was a little feather minnow, with a blue head and Barred Rock feathers. I held my cast until a number of snook were at the surface chasing minnows, then flipped the bug right in among them, skittering it over them as rapidly as I could manage. It worked, and the same trick has worked a number of times since. I believe that the fish simply confused the skittering bug with the skipping minnows and grabbed it in their haste to beat each other to the punch.

There are no special tackle requirements for snook fishing. You can use standard fresh water gear—only perhaps a little more of it than you'd use for bass or pike. For fishing the beaches or canals where the water is open and relatively free of obstructions, all you need is your light casting, spinning, or fly outfit. Plenty of line is in order where the fish have room to run, and by plenty I mean at least one hundred yards. When it comes to fishing a mangrove shore line, you might want to use beefier gear, say twenty-pound casting line or eight-pound spinning line. Not that such gear will enable you to prevent a big snook's plowing mangrove roots if he decides to do so, but at least you might feel more secure with it. Actually, the best way to get a big snook out of the mangroves is to make him think you don't want him to come out. Don't try to bull him right away; just lead him gently, using either no pressure at all or just enough to keep a belly out of the line. After you've coaxed him out a way, pour it on. Oh, you'll lose plenty of snook, and lures too, but that's what makes snook fishing great.

There's only one more thing you have to know to be a snook fisherman, and that's the snook's generic name, *Centropomus*. *Centropomus* means "spur plus cover," and it's the scientist's way of warning you to use a wire leader. Snook, in other words, have razor sharp, saw-toothed spurs on their gill covers, and they can slice fishing lines with the greatest of ease. I like a light, braided stainless steel leader about a foot long, either with or without a nylon cover.

Snook are resident natives in South Florida, active the year 'round. Late spring, early summer, and fall are perhaps the most productive fishing times for them, but you can always find snook if you want them. All of the rivers, creeks and canals in South Florida are good snook water, and plenty of them are to be found in the surf from Fort Myers Beach to Naples. The surest way to get 'em is to visit Marco Island or Everglades City and hire a guide to fish the Ten Thousand Islands. That, my friends, is snook country!

As the man from Wisconsin said, "There's something about a snook." Something—I can't say exactly what—but something that gets you. I dare you to try 'em.

CHAPTER **6**

Jacks Are Tough Cookies

M Y STREAMER vanished in a heavy swirl, and I automatically raised the rod to set the hook. The tip
snapped down violently, and the rod was nearly torn from my
grasp. A high-pitched scream of agony came from the reel,
while the line sizzled through the water like a red-hot knife.
"Big snook!" I yelled to C. J. Nielsen, wanting any moral
support he could offer me. (Too much fish on too little tackle
calls for some sort of cheering section.) The fly line appeared
suspended in midair as more and more of the black ten-pound-
test nylon backing sped through the guides.

We were fishing inside the fence enclosing the water-
control locks at Ortona, and the situation seemed impossible,
as the fence would prevent my following the fish downstream.
When the reel arbor began to show through the spooled line,
I held the straining rod as far over the fence as possible, waiting for something to break, but hoping the "snook" would
turn.

I was sure the fish had me whipped, when C. J. appeared on the outside of the fence. "Gimme the rod!" he yelled. "Don't bust him off!"

We managed the transfer all right, and I lit out for the gate of the enclosure. When I arrived at the scene of action, C. J., rod, and fish were still connected; and I again took over. Running and stumbling along the rocky bank, I got some line back on the spool. With nearly a mile of unobstructed river bank ahead of me—unless you'd call cottonmouth moccasins obstructions—I felt sure I could land my fish, but he gave me some anxious moments when he decided to try scraping the fly from his jaw on the opposite bank 125 yards away. When the runs finally began to slow down a bit, my suspicions were aroused. That steady throbbing, the absence of jumps or surface action of any kind, were not what was to be expected from a snook. "Still," I thought, "lots of snook refuse to jump, especially when hooked on a fly; and maybe the throbbing is from my aching wrist." A quarter-mile below the fence I had my answer.

Too tired to do more than feebly wave his fins, my fish lay on his side and allowed me to beach him. The sight of him was a great disappointment, but I could not help feeling a strong admiration for his power and determination. "Damn jack," I called to C. J. " 'Bout six pounds."

C. J. glanced at his watch as I got a grip on the jack's tail and hoisted him up. "Thirty-seven minutes," he said. "No wonder you thought you had a big snook!"

I photographed and released the jack, then lit a cigarette, sat down, and flexed my rod. It was so soft it would not straighten of its own accord when I put a slight bend in it. I carefully straightened it out and laid it in the shade to cool off and recover. That jack had given the rod the most severe beating it had ever received. It was the first time in my experience that a high-grade bamboo rod had softened under the heat of battle.

After a rest of ten minutes my wrist felt a lot better, and the rod had recovered most of its zip. Now I was ready to get that big snook!

Staying outside the fence this time, I resumed casting the Black Ghost. I allowed it to sink for several seconds before starting the first retrieve, and starting the retrieve was as far as I got. The line was jerked from my left hand, and the rod was abruptly snapped into a parabolic curve.

"Whatcha got?" asked C. J.

"Big snook!" I informed him.

This time I was able to keep backing on the reel by skipping along the bank with the downstream runs and staying within my tackle's range of the fish. This one was a snook all right, and a good one! There could be no doubt; only a big, head-shaking snook could jar my wrist as this fish did. He even dived deep into the current and sounded (an action typical of large snook on light tackle), and only sharp tapping on the reel seat would get him moving again. Not until the six-ounce rod had begun to feel like a thirty-pound sledge hammer, and my wrist had become numb, did the fish show signs of weakening. Now I had him coming. By pumping him with the rod and spooling the line so gained, I brought him to within a rod's length of the shore.

C. J. came down the bank to help me land him. "What'd'ya think he'll go?" he asked.

"Well," I said, "the biggest snook I've ever landed on a

fly outfit went seven and a half pounds, but he wasn't in the same league with this one. He'll go ten pounds easy!"

Under the steady pressure of bamboo, the fish came to the surface. C. J.'s roar of laughter echoed up and down the Caloosahatchee Valley. You guessed it, another jack—a five-pounder this time.

"Ya musta' horsed him," C. J. remarked. "He only lasted twenty-two minutes."

I lost no time in clipping off the fly and disjointing my rod.

"Aintcha gonna' fish?" asked C. J.

"And take a chance on becoming involved with another jack? Hell, no!" I bitterly replied. "Enough is enough! How much fishin' can a guy stand?"

Now, I'm as avid a fisherman as ever cast a lure, the real screwball type who never knows when to quit. I'll pound miles of rugged trout stream from dawn to dark, and be up before daylight the next morning raring to pound it again. I'll sling spinning lures through several turns of the tide without even a break for lunch, while my bigger and huskier partners plead to go home and get some rest. I'll fight bass, or bonefish, or barracuda, or bluegills for ten hours a day, seven days a week, with undiminished enthusiasm. But every time I blunder into a school of crevalle jacks with fly or spinning tackle, I wind up hollering uncle.

Jacks play too darned rough. Even singly, they'd be bad enough, but they usually don't travel singly. When you whip one jack, you've got to take on his buddies one by one . . . unless you've got enough sense to pull a strategic withdrawal. The first one isn't so bad. His vicious head-shaking, powerful runs, and long, unrelenting fight win your respect and deep

Manny Eisfeld admires a six-pound snook he caught on a rapidly worked spinning size darter. The location: Chokoloskee Bay near Everglades City.

Casting a mangrove shoreline for snook in the Ten Thousand Islands. This is snook country!

Ten-pound jack crevalle taken on spinning tackle off Key Largo.

Manny Eisfeld of Miami with a two-pound ladyfish. These fish are unbelievably hard fighters for their size.

John Herbert took this spotted sea trout on a very small home-made spinning bucktail.

Manny Eisfeld nets a spotted sea trout in the lower Caloosahatchee River. A landing net should always be used on trout if you want to boat a respectable percentage of the ones you hook.

Eight-pound channel bass taken by the author on a spinning bucktail near Pine Island on Florida's lower west coast.

The great barracuda, in spite of his ferocious appearance, is an even-tempered fis 'Cudas strike for food, not out of sheer cussedness. (*Photographed at Marine Studios*

admiration. You release him gently, tenderly, and compliment him for so gallant a fight. You make another cast, and you've hardly started your retrieve when a smashing strike snaps your rod into a bow. For a second or two you think you've got a record-size weakfish, snook, or channel bass, but then you recognize the powerful pulsating throb of another jack. This one seems to fight even harder and longer than the first, and your wrists are beginning to ache when you finally bring him to the net. You release this one, too, but not so gently. Another cast brings another jolting strike, and now your wrists ache before the jack even gets warmed up. You begin to wish that you'd stopped for a cigarette after that last one, but you steel yourself to the task and fight the jack. You fight him until you begin praying for him to break off. Before you land him you have to ward off the temptation to tighten your drag and break the line, but you remind yourself that you've never purposely broken off a fish and won't start now. You do net him eventually, after spending the final several minutes trying to get his head up with one numb hand, while holding the net in the other—while the jack plods slowly back and forth just out of reach. By now you no longer recognize jacks as gallant fighters. They are sadistic bullies. Brutes. Damjackfish!

Every fisherman should catch a sizable crevalle jack, just for the educational value. Even the little ones will enlighten you. You'll never know how much power per pound can be packed into fish flesh until you've caught a jack. They're not hard to hook, as they have a devil-may-care attitude toward life and will frequently hit just about any lure you feel like showing them.

The common crevalle jack is one of the toughest of the entire rugged jack tribe, with muscular power and endurance that no other inshore fish can match. Pound for pound, the common jack can outpull and outlast any of the more glamorous game fish without even extending himself. But he's not generally considered a great game fish, and probably never will be.

Crevalle jacks are actually too tough to be great game fish. By that, I mean that catching them can run into work rather than sport. The crevalle should be a light-tackle fish, as his average weight runs only a couple of pounds in inshore waters and perhaps five to ten pounds offshore. Mere average crevalle jacks, however, can take the fun out of light-tackle fishing by making it such a gruelling job. Big ones are murder. Jacks have made me holler uncle many times, and I've no doubt that they'll do it again.

Perhaps you're wondering what a "jack" is. Throughout the South, the Eastern or chain pickerel is called a jack. This chapter is not about pickerel. The jack we're considering is a salt-water fish, who, like the snook and tarpon, frequently makes long journeys into fresh water out of pure wanderlust. He's pretty much a warm-water fish and is very abundant in the seas, bays, and rivers of southern Florida. Ichthyologists call him *Caranx hippos*; the things anglers call him shouldn't happen to a dog—not even to a streamlined bulldog with fins.

Down here in Florida we have some pretty respectable game fish. Nearly all of them have received copious amounts of well-deserved publicity. Anglers all over the country know of our flashy tarpon, our bizarre sailfish, our fabulous bonefish, our vicious barracuda, and our tackle-busting snook. Our huge bass are world famous. Yet the toughest of them all, the jack crevalle, is comparatively unknown outside of his immediate range. Hold it now! I didn't say that the jack is the best of

Florida's game fish; I said *"the toughest,"* and I'll argue *that* point until the Gulf of Mexico freezes over!

Along Florida's lower west coast he's frequently called "damjackfish" (one word). I once hung one from the Naples municipal pier with a light bass casting outfit. My tackle consisted of a five-and-a-half-foot light-action glass rod, regular level-wind casting reel, and ten-pound-test nylon line. For forty-five minutes the jack and I tussled. A sizable crowd had gathered to see what sort of monster fish I had. When I finally worked my quarry to the surface, the word "damjackfish" circulated through the crowd, the crowd disappeared, and I had a hard time getting someone to operate the landing net for me. That Naples jack weighed fourteen pounds. A snook of similar size taken on comparable tackle would have caused a mild sensation; yet the jack, which probably could have outlasted and outpulled a snook of twice his weight, was considered trash. Small wonder he hasn't received the publicity and reputation our "glamour fishes" have.

The crevalle is far and away the most commonly encountered member of the jack family in North American waters. In the northerly parts of his range, he is a fish of offshore waters not ordinarily sought by the average angler. Along the entire coast of Florida, however, jacks are much more accessible to the ordinary fisherman. They run in the surf, inlets, bays and rivers, often in large schools that churn the water to a froth in frenzied feeding sprees. The schools travel rapidly when foraging for food, and it is very difficult to keep up with them. If you can manage to get any sort of lure into a fast-moving bunch of jacks, it is practically impossible to get it out again without a strike.

As a rule, however, it pays to ignore the fast-moving

schools, and fish for the strays and small pods instead. There will nearly always be a few jacks around every channel-marker, creek mouth, sand or oyster bar or swash channel; and it's much more practical to concentrate on these fish than to try to keep up with the travelling schools.

Jacks have a decided weakness for yellow lures, particularly feather jigs, spinning bucktails, and streamer flies. They like the same sort of whippy retrieve that most other salt-water fish find attractive, but if you want to fish especially for jacks, work the lure a bit faster than normal.

At times, crevalles gather in large schools and hang around given areas for extended periods to feed on finger mullet, small menhaden, or other schooling forage fish. When this occurs, the jacks become extremely selective and refuse to have any truck with the lures they normally break their necks over. Such selective schools are frequently encountered just outside inlets or passes, and in the lower reaches of tidal rivers. The best way to catch these temperamental feeders is to use a small surface plug, preferably spinning size, and spot-cast it to rising fish. When you see a mullet or menhaden start skipping along the surface, try to hit him with the plug. Start your retrieve the instant it strikes the water, and work it just as rapidly and erratically as you can. The idea is to confuse the jack into thinking your plug is the fish he was chasing . . . and it seems to work. Color or style of the plug is unimportant, so long as it stays on the surface and makes plenty of commotion.

Closely related to the crevalle jack are the blue runner, the yellow (or bar) jack, and the runner. Of these fish the blue runner is the most common, and his range closely co-incides with that of the crevalle. The yellow jack and runner, however, are found in significant numbers only in the Florida Keys. All are every bit as tough as the crevalle for their size, but average somewhat smaller. They strike the same lures and feed in the same slashing manner as the crevalle, but they do not range into inside waters to the extent that the crevalle does.

King of the jack tribe in Florida—or anywhere else, for that matter—is the big and brawny amberjack. Fairly common from North Carolina southward, the amberjack is most plentiful in the offshore waters of the entire Florida coast line.

My very first jack was a baby amberjack, a mere infant weighing about as much as a prewar hamburger, and just as full of mustard. I was casting a small clothespin plug for young channel bass off a well-known fishing pier and having a wonderful time with them, too. Then that doggone little amberjack horned in. When he hit, I shouted to all the fishermen on the pier to get their lines out of the way and give me room. "Big fish on!" I hollered, "Get your dam' lines in!" The fish bored into run after run, lunging back and forth and jarring my wrists with bulldog shakes every time he changed directions. After a minute or two I was able to keep him in check pretty well, but he just wouldn't give ground. I became more and more convinced that he was a very big fish, liable to take off and strip me of line at any time. I poured it on him, using all the power my rod could exert, and finally he began to tire. With a series of long, strenuous pumps of the casting rod, I bulled the fish in to the pier. As he came to the surface, still feebly waving his tail in an effort to continue the fight, the pier rang with derisive laughter.

One understanding gentleman standing at my side gave me a kind smile. "Your first jack?" he asked.

I nodded. "It happens every day," he consoled. "Everybody acts silly first time he hangs a jack."

That amberjack measured only eighteen inches, but he gave a better account of himself than any other fish I had caught on casting tackle up to that time. Much better, in fact, than largemouths of seven pounds and smallmouths of four!

When you consider that amberjacks average about thirty-five to forty pounds and run up to one hundred in Florida waters, you can imgaine what you're up against when you stick a hook in one. Not long ago, while fooling around on the edge of the Gulf Stream off Key Largo with spinning tackle, I spotted a small school of five- or six-pound yellow jacks lying under a patch of floating gulfweed. I flipped my bucktail alongside the weed, and as I started my retrieve the jacks eased out behind the lure. Suddenly a massive shape charged through the school of yellow jacks and took the bucktail away from them. An amberjack! A four-foot amberjack that could give any big-game fisherman a bad time, hooked on a size 1 Upperman bucktail, four-ounce rod, and six-pound-test line. At first, the amberjack didn't seem to realize that he was hooked, for he merely swam around at the surface opening his mouth and shaking his head for a while. When he did wake up, it was hell-to-tell-the-captain! Diving at about a forty-five-degree angle, he headed for bottom and didn't stop until he'd taken nearly 250 yards of line. Then he sulked and defied me to pump him up. Believe me, big amberjacks do not pump easily on spinning tackle, but I tried. With the handle braced under my forearm, I gave the powerful Sila-Flex rod all the bend it would take and then rocked on it and plucked at the line. For one hour and thirty-five minutes I gave that amberjack all the pressure my tackle would stand, and finally he decided to come up for a run. Then the hook pulled out, which was just as well, as the physical strain in the hot sun had me nauseated and on the point of collapse. Some day, I'm going to land a big amberjack spinning, but I don't think I can do it on a flat calm, sunny day on the Gulf Stream.

While occasional schools of baby amberjacks come inshore, the larger fish usually stick pretty close to the outer reefs near the edge of the Gulf Stream, in water from thirty to over one hundred feet deep. They prefer the heavy, craggy reefs with abrupt ledges and coral caves, and where you can find such reefs in Florida you'll surely find amberjack. Sometimes they venture a short distance out into the Gulf Stream to feed around patches of floating gulfweed that shelter small fish.

Amberjack fishing is a rather specialized field, and if you want to catch one your best bet is to charter out of Panama City, Miami, or anywhere in the Keys for the purpose. While amberjacks are taken with some regularity by routine Gulf Stream trollers, drift-fishing on the outer reefs with live grunts is a much better way to get them—a sure way, if your skipper knows his business.

Amberjacks unquestionably reach much greater weights than the current world record of 119 pounds, 8 ounces. A crew of red snapper fishermen working out of Panama City, Florida, hand-lined one weighing 146 pounds, but stated that they'd lost several considerably bigger. Too tough to handle, even with nylon sash-cord hand lines! Most of the unstoppable fish hooked from time to time by offshore anglers in the Gulf of Mexico are probably huge amberjacks.

The jack family is a large one, represented by members in the tropical and temperate seas in all hemispheres of the world. Some of the jacks, like the scads and bumpers, are very small forage fish; while others, like the amberjack, Pacific yellowtail and Hawaiian ulua, reach the big-game size. Some jacks are surface dwellers, while others swim deep. Some branches of the jack tribe are hardly fit to eat, while others, including the fabulous pompano, are meat for the gods. The jack family is, in fact, far too large and varied to cover completely in a single chapter, but there is one general statement that can be applied to all of them. They are the roughest, toughest, most powerful family of fish in or out of the sea. Big or small, bottom-grubbers or surface-feeders, inedible or ambrosia, all of the jacks are fighting fish.

Jacks are so plentiful in Florida that it's almost impossible to do any amount of salt-water fishing there without catching one. They are ready strikers on practically any kind of natural bait or artificial lure you'd think of using, and they are seldom temperamental or selective.

Maybe you'll despise them for the bullies they are. You'll perhaps begrudge them the large amount of your fishing time their long fights consume. You might be after "eatin' fish," and cuss jacks because they're not. You may not like their gruelling, nonaerial fights, which make you think you're tied to record snook or channel bass. But you've got to admit that jacks are tough cookies.

CHAPTER 7

The Tarpon's Little Cousin

ONE DAY a few years ago Manny Eisfeld and I were drifting the sea trout flats off Iona Cove in the Lower Caloosahatchee River, casting spinning bucktails and catching an occasional trout, pinfish, and small snapper. By no stretch of the imagination could the fishing be called exciting, but spinning was new to us then, and any fish we caught seemed worth while just for the novelty of the thing. Then Manny's reel drag suddenly began to sing. I quickly netted a trout I'd been playing and laid down my rod.

"Need any help?" I asked jokingly.

"Start the motor!" Manny shouted, as if trying to make himself heard above the whine of his reel. "My line's almost gone!"

I yanked the cord, and we roared after the fish, but Manny's reel didn't even slow down. Suddenly, his rod snapped straight as the fish spun in a tight U turn and headed back with undiminished speed. By the time I had shut off the motor, the fish was almost at the boat, and Manny's line was bellied out in a slack U fifty yards long.

"This fish must be rocket propelled," Manny exclaimed. "I can't keep up with him."

A twisting sliver of silver shot into the air, hit the water with rockets still going full blast, and again the reel screamed as the monofilament hissed through the guides.

Manny's face was a perfect picture of incredulity as he beheld the fish. "That little thing isn't doing this; it's my imagination!" he exclaimed.

"That 'little thing,' Manny, is a big ladyfish," I laughed. "The most underrated fish in the world!"

Several runs and jumps later the ladyfish allowed itself to be netted, unhooked and released. It weighed perhaps two and one-half pounds. Two and a half pounds of fantastically competent fish.

"Whew," breathed Manny, "and I thought bonefish could fight."

"All of the bones we've tangled with went four or five pounds or better," I remarked. "Get ahold of a ladyfish that size, and . . ."

"No," Manny interrupted, "you get ahold of a ladyfish that size; I'm not sure I'd want one."

I've hooked a king-size ladyfish only once, a few years ago. I was spending some time in the Florida Keys with a fly rod and stop watch, trying to measure the speed of running bonefish. One night, after an afternoon of bonefishing, I heard fish popping by a bridge near my cabin and couldn't resist going out to toss a fly at them. My first cast was greeted with a slashing hit typical of the strike of a ladyfish. In the lights of a passing car I saw the fish clearly on its first jump, and a ladyfish it was, a really big one of five or six pounds. Then came the run, a marathon sprint that was hyphenated by five jumps, but nevertheless stripped my reel of a forty-yard fly line and one hundred yards of backing in a matter of seconds. Fortunately, the break came at the leader tippet.

Most ladyfish do not run so far in a straight line; but when they do, they really make a job of it. Regrettably, I did not put the stop watch on that Keys ladyfish, but I feel certain that the fastest bonefish in the world couldn't have matched the speed of her 140–yard run. I succeeded in getting the clockings on bonefish, and one of these days I hope to be lucky enough to get some ladyfish speed figures for comparison. I'm betting on the little lady.

Speaking of bonefish, books on fish often caution us that the ladyfish (*Elops saurus*) should not be confused with the high and mighty bonefish (*Albula vulpes*)—the implication being that the ladyfish is small potatoes. Actually, there is little danger of confusing the two, for ladyfish are much more versatile fighters, harder to hook and harder to land. Any bonefish that happens to be mistaken for a ladyfish should feel flattered, yet the bonefish has an enormous reputation and the ladyfish is almost unknown.

I'll never understand why the wiry little ladyfish hasn't received the recognition she so thoroughly deserves. (Probably about half the ladyfish are he's, but it seems awkward to refer to them in anything other than the female gender.) Size considered, she is the fastest, strongest, and most acrobatic fish in Florida waters. A broad statement, but if you think it's an exaggeration, you obviously have never hooked a ladyfish of two pounds or better on a fly or spinning rod.

Her fight is breathtakingly furious and without any sort of letup until she's completely exhausted. Like her famous glamour-boy cousin, the tarpon, the ladyfish does everything a game fish is expected to do—and does it exceedingly well. She strikes hard, sprints fast, jumps high and often, and runs with determination and power. If her endurance seems a bit less than that of stubborn plodders like the jacks, it should be borne in mind that the ladyfish packs more fighting action into five minutes than most other fish manage to produce in an hour. She's so fast that it's a physical impossibility to keep a tight line on her, and her hook-throwing ability matches that of her tarpon cousin.

Yes, the ladyfish is a little cousin of the mighty tarpon, bearing the same family name, *Elopidae*. She's a lot like the tarpon in several respects, and I like to think of her as a tarpon in concentrated form. Her sudden, gill-rattling jumps, startling change of pace, and rapid acceleration are tarponistic to a degree that even the tarpon himself cannot achieve. Her silvery complexion and racy form are suggestive of the tarpon's appearance; but the ladyfish is more elongate, less compressed in the body, and has much smaller scales than the tarpon.

Ichthyologists, for some obscure reason, insist on referring to the ladyfish as a "ten-pounder," an ill-chosen alias if there ever was one. I'd certainly like to see a ten-pound ladyfish; but there is little likelihood that *Elops saurus* ever reaches this weight in American waters. In some circles, the ladyfish is tagged "big-eyed herring," a misnomer because, big eyes or not, she is definitely no herring. "Ladyfish" is the most commonly used name, and a most fitting name for this sleek and dainty finster. Around Miami, ladyfish are sometimes called "chiro," a name also used to some extent in the Keys. Then, too, I've heard them called by names that need not be mentioned here.

The unmentionable names for ladyfish are generally coined by meat fishermen who understandably hate to sacrifice expensive live shrimp for inedible fish. Perhaps ladyfish aren't actually inedible, but eating them is impractical for the simple reason that the energy expended in removing their bones is greater than the food value realized from their meager flesh. As far as I'm concerned, this is a point in the ladyfish's favor, for she is in no danger of being depleted by commercial fishermen or meat-hog "sportsmen." Ladyfish are abundant even in this day and age, and probably always will be.

When you happen upon a school of actively feeding ladyfish, you're in for some of the fastest fishing action imaginable. Their zippy, jarring strikes come with staccato rapidity as they forget to be ladylike in their haste to beat each other to the lure. When hungry they are even wilder and faster than usual, grabbing the lure on the run and racing away with it as if afraid their sisters might take it away from them. On feeling the hook they go into a series of unbelievably violent tantrums and hurl themselves about in a completely uninhibited manner until they're exhausted. They somehow contrive to jump while running and to run while jumping, a trick no other fish can perform. For swiftly paced, concentrated action, there is no fishing like ladyfishing.

One night several years ago C. J. Nielsen and I were fooling around one of the bridges at Fort Myers Beach in hopes of getting a few spotted sea trout on fly tackle. We waited for the incoming tide in hopes that it would bring shrimp, which in turn would bring the trout to the surface.

Finally, we began to see flashes of phosphorus in the dark water, and the popping and slashing of feeding fish began.

"Here they are," C. J. exclaimed. "What shall we use, streamer or popper?"

"I'll try a streamer; you use a popper," I suggested. "Then we'll find out which they prefer."

I've always been pretty good at tying flies on in the dark, and I had my first cast out before C. J. finished fiddling around with his knot. My streamer had no more than hit the water when my reel developed an acute case of screaming meemies. There was a sudden jump, the sound of rattling gill covers, and the fish was off.

"Lost one, C. J.," I said.

"So I heard," he answered. "What in heck kind of a trout was that?"

I didn't get a chance to answer him, for another fish hit while I was reeling in to check my fly. Again my reel screamed, sounding almost like a cat with its tail caught in a door. With the reel wailing and the rod bowing and quivering like a reed in a hurricane, I could feel and hear my fish jumping. The jumps came in such rapid succession that I couldn't tell when the fish was in the water and when it was in the air.

Then I heard another reel break into song and realized that C. J. had finally found the eye of his bug hook. We began to speculate about the identity of our fish.

"Do flying fish hit flies?" C. J. quipped. "Mine's out of the water most of the time."

"So's mine," I chuckled, "but I don't think there are any flying fish here."

"Well, they're darn sure not trout," said C. J.

"Mine's whipped now," I said as I picked up the landing

net. "I'll land him in the dark; a light might scare the rest of them away."

I knew it couldn't be anything but a ladyfish. Nothing else with fins could put up such a violent scrap. I reached down and scooped up about two pounds of ladyfish, and a few moments later C. J. did the same thing. The school stayed around the bridge for about an hour, and that was the fastest and most spectacular hour of fly fishing I have ever experienced. Every cast brought at least one strike, and if a strike was missed another ladyfish had the fly before a back cast could be made. Our reels actually and literally became hot from the continued torture of the screeching runs those little two-pound fish made. We never did see any trout that night, but as C. J. remarked when I hinted that it was too bad we didn't get any trout to take home, "All the trout in the Gulf couldn't have given us that much fun!"

Ladyfish are said to range as far north as Cape Cod, Massachusetts, but they are extremely rare north of the Carolinas and not really plentiful in any state but Florida. In South Florida ladyfish are likely to be encountered in any kind of water, even fresh water if it leads directly to salt. They are probably more numerous in the Gulf of Mexico and its tributaries from St. Petersburg south than anywhere else in the United States. Other hot ladyfish spots are Florida's lower east coast, especially the bridges of Biscayne Bay, and inside waters of the Keys.

The biggest concentration of ladyfish I've ever seen gathered on the north side of Little Shell Island in the lower Caloosahatchee River a couple of years ago and stayed around for over two weeks. There's no telling how many ladyfish were in that school, but they covered well over an acre of water surface when feeding on schools of top minnows that happened by. There were so many ladyfish that it was impossible to catch anything else in the area until they moved out. Meat fishermen found the situation unbearable, but ladyfish addicts like me were in hog heaven while it lasted.

Few people fish expressly for ladyfish, but these fish are so plentiful that they are likely to be taken accidentally in greater numbers than the "eating" fish being purposely sought. Feeding at all water levels, from top to bottom, ladyfish will take any of the commonly used natural baits, and thousands of them are caught on old-style salt-water tackle consisting of the usual stiff rod, big star-drag reel, hawser-type line, heavy sinker, and natural bait. This hasn't done much for their reputation as game fish, for what can a fish averaging one pound in weight and given to aerial exhibitions be expected to do against such tackle? When she comes up to jump, she's heaved into the boat or onto the bridge. On fly, spinning, or light casting tackle, however, the little lady is dynamite on a short fuse.

A fly outfit is the most practical tackle for ladyfish, not only because flies are their favorite lures, but also because their average weight of about one pound places them in the ultra-light-tackle category. Probably the most consistent lure is a relatively small streamer or bucktail, preferably in white or yellow on a size 2 to 1/0 hook. Fly-rod poppers, too, are excellent; their noisy action calls ladyfish from considerable distances. Both streamers and poppers should be retrieved rapidly for these speedy little fish.

Just as fitting as the fly rod for ladyfishing is a light spinning outfit. Small weighted bucktails and jigs in the one-eighth-ounce to one-fourth-ounce class, the new tiny top water spinning plugs, and all of the European-type spinning lures are items of considerable attraction to ladyfish. As a rule, these too should be fished moderately fast for best results. The sudden startling jolt with which a ladyfish hits a rapidly retrieved spinning lure is a long-to-be-remembered angling thrill.

For a real picnic with ladyfish, try a double spinning lure rig as described in Chapter One—but be sure you have a good supply of lures on hand. I once laughed myself silly watching Johnny Herbert lose ten spinning jigs in five casts while trying to land a ladyfish double header. Johnny would painstakingly rig up, make a cast, and then cuss a blue streak as two ladyfish would latch on, take off in opposite directions and tear the rig apart. At that time, however, neither Johnny nor I knew how to rig two lures properly. We seldom lose lures to ladyfish these days, even with a double rig.

Bait-casting is not quite so well adapted to ladyfishing as either fly-fishing or spinning. Most standard casting lures are too large to be very attractive to ladyfish of average size, although the big ones will sometimes wallop the largest of plugs. Probably the best casting lure is a small block tin squid reeled as speedily as possible. Small feather jigs are good, as are top water plugs in the one-fourth- to one-half-ounce weight class. Especially effective is a very small spoon, such as a size oo Drone or o Reflecto, fished as for mackerel or shad—with a clincher sinker above the leader for casting weight. Another good rig is a trailer fly fastened behind a top water plug with about twelve to fifteen inches of monfilament nylon. The plug attracts them, and they hit the fly.

The natural diet of ladyfish consists mainly of crustaceans and minnows of all sorts, with shrimp their special weakness.

They forage in loose schools and seem to feed noncooperatively, rather than herding and surrounding their prey as jacks and bluefish do. Rarely feeding selectively, they don't object to mixing shrimp with minnows or minnows with small crabs. When their feed bags are on, they'll generally take a whack at any bait or small lure that happens by. Neither wary, nor shy, nor temperamental, ladyfish do not insist on masterful casting demonstrations or subtle presentations of the lure. They'll strike for anyone who can cast well enough to hit the water occasionally.

Ladyfish feed in inlets and passes, along the beaches of the Gulf coast, in the channels of lower reaches of rivers, over the grass flats and oyster bars in the bays, and around the mouths of the smaller, mangrove-lined creeks. They are most active on a strong incoming tide, and seem to operate on a twenty-four-hour schedule, feeding even more freely at night than they do during daylight hours.

The next time you're in Florida on a line-wetting expedition, do yourself a favor and give some attention to the ultra-game little ladyfish. You'll find her at any season of the year in South Florida, ever ready, willing and able to sock your fly or spinning lure harder than you'd believe possible for such a small fish. Compare every phase of her savage fight with the combined tactics of all the other game fish you've ever caught. You'll find that the ladyfish can strike like a barracuda, pull like a jack, run like a bonefish, jump like a tarpon, and maneuver better than any of 'em. The tarpon's little cousin is quite a gal.

CHAPTER **8**

The Sea Trout Is a Boxer

ONE EVENING after supper Wes Henson dropped by the house and told me he had a serious problem. "Here it is Saturday night," he groaned, "and I still haven't been able to catch enough fish for that fish-fry I'm throwing Wednesday. The bass aren't hitting, and what bream I've been able to catch are too small."

"Well, you've still got tomorrow," I said.

"Yeah, and tomorrow's all I *have* got. That's why I came over to see if you'd take me to one of your secret salt-water places, where we'd be sure to catch some fish."

"Heck, Wes," I laughed, "I don't have any secret places, but I do think we may be able to get a mess of fish. What time shall I pick you up?"

Shortly after sunup the next morning we launched the boat at Punta Rassa and headed for the nearest sea trout flat. By nine o'clock our icebox contained enough trout for three or four fish fries, and Wes' problem was solved. "Now let's go find some real fish," I yawned. "These doggone trout bore me."

I was only half-kidding. Sea trout do bore me, and they'd bore you, too, if they'd topped your annual catch of fresh- and salt-water fish for several years in a row. When you've caught seven or eight hundred, you've caught 'em all, but they sure come in handy when there's a fish fry deadline to meet!

Sea trout, or spotted weakfish, are unquestionably the most plentiful of all Florida's game fish, fresh or salt water. Ranging from Pensacola to the Upper Keys and over the entire length of the Florida east coast, these fish are the bread and butter of hundreds of commercial fishermen and the old standby of thousands of Florida anglers. They are especially numerous in the Bay of Florida and along the Gulf coast, particularly around Cedar Keys, Tampa Bay, Charlotte Harbor, and Pine Island Sound. The biggest specimens haunt the lagoons of the middle east coast, the stretch from Melbourne south to Palm Beach being world famous for the size of its spotted sea trout.

Spotted sea trout are especially fond of grassy bottoms in bays, lagoons, and sounds, in water from two to six feet deep. With the rising tide they range over shallow grass flats to feed on shrimp and minnows, dropping back to the deeper flats and holes when the tide recedes. At times, they feed along the Gulf beaches, congregating around small inlets and passes where the food supply is greatest. During periods of very hot or very cool weather, sea trout may leave the shallow flats for deeper water, but as soon as the weather straightens out they return again to their beloved flats. Over the northern half of Florida many trout enter the rivers and creeks in late fall to spend the winter in the deep channels, but in the southern part of the state they roam the flats the year 'round.

Along the Gulf coast of South Florida, another of the weakfishes is sometimes found in fair numbers. Known scientifically as *Cynoscion arenarius*, his common name is sand sea trout. Natives simply call him gray trout. This fish is a much harder fighter for his size than the spotted sea trout, but he runs considerably smaller. A two-pound sand trout is a real whopper.

He feeds pretty close to the bottom as a rule, and prefers deeper water than his freckled cousin. Sand trout are nearly always confined to sand-bottomed channels, rarely venturing onto the grass flats or bars. They may be caught by fishing small jigs right on the bottom in bay swash channels and larger passes of Florida's lower west coast. They like a very slow retrieve as a rule, and will pick up a jig that is simply dragged slowly over the bottom with no action imparted by the rod or reel.

Sand trout have no spots, are a brassy silver on the sides, and are tan with purplish reflections on the back. They are of little importance either commercially or as a game fish, and I've discussed them here merely to aid you with the identification, should you run into them.

The spotted sea trout's other correct names are *Cynoscion nebulosus* and spotted weakfish, but most everybody just calls him a trout. Averaging a little over a pound, he is one of four weakfishes indigenous to Atlantic and Gulf waters, all of which are closely related to such Pacific nifties as the California white sea bass and the king-size totuava. Most of the weakfishes are fairly hard fighters, but the spotted sea trout, I'm sorry to say, is not. He doesn't have to be a hard fighter for two reasons: first, he always has his gang with him; and second, he's not a bad boxer.

In spite of his lack of punching power, the spotted sea trout is one of the most popular salt-water fish among artificial-lure addicts of Florida. A handsome fellow, he strikes hard and fast, and puts up an interesting—if light—scrap. His fight, consisting of a series of short, fast lunges interspersed with considerable surface wallowing, earns him his freedom a good share of the time. And since his fancy boxing tactics enable him to shake the hook in better style than most of the hard-fighting fish can manage, far be it from me to criticize him. He has a tender mouth, and he evidently knows it. Who ever heard of a successful wide-open slugger with a glass jaw? And, in all fairness, it must be admitted that trout become pretty fair battlers when they reach a weight of five pounds or so.

While spotted sea trout are not exactly exciting fish, you can sometimes have a lot of fun playing with them. C. J. Nielsen and I once celebrated a Fourth of July holiday by tying up to a channel-marker off Punta Rassa and catching trout double-headers as fast as we could unhook them. Such ridiculously easy fishing quickly became boring, and soon we were putting all sorts of restrictions on ourselves to make catching the trout a little harder. First we mashed down the barbs on our hooks and made a rule that it was double or nothing; if a cast brought only one trout to the boat we had to turn him loose. Even this was too easy, and eventually we cut our hooks off just behind the barbs, leaving only the bend . . . and darned if we didn't manage to boat a few trout!

Tackle for sea trout should be light, for practical as well as sporting reasons. There's no surer way to lose a trout than to horse him, for his soft mouth tears very easily. Light equipment automatically discourages horsing tactics. From a sporting point of view, only the lightest of tackle can give sea trout a chance to show you what they can do. By a remarkable coincidence, the most sporting tackle for sea trout is also the most practical from the standpoint of meat in the pot! This is not true with regard to most fish.

If there was ever a fish for which fresh-water spinning tackle was made to order, that fish is the sea trout. You could travel around the world seeking a perfect spinning fish, but you couldn't find a better one than sea trout. Or you could spend a lifetime devising a fishing outfit especially for spotted sea trout, but you could never invent a better one than light spinning gear. Of course, this doesn't imply that bait-casting or fly tackle aren't suitable for sea trout. Actually, any sort of light fresh-water gear is excellent, but don't use conventional salt-water tackle unless you're just kidding.

Sea trout are ready strikers, bless 'em, and natural bait is seldom—if ever—needed for these fish. While they will eagerly hit live shrimp, minnows, or cut bait, they'll take artificial lures equally well . . . if the lures are fished the way they happen to want 'em. They like small lures—smaller, in fact, than the average fisherman thinks of using. My good friend and spin-fishing buddy Johnny Herbert has had amazing success on trout with a tiny homemade weighted bucktail tied on a size 10 hook. He uses it in tandem behind a conventional jig such as a number 1 Upperman. I haven't tried Johnny's midget, but I have fooled plenty of sea trout with a very small bucktail tied on a size 4 hook, over-all length about an inch and a half. These little lures work wonders when trout are supposed to be off their feed.

Day in, day out, it's hard to beat conventional bucktail

jigs as sea trout lures. They'll take trout over a wider range of water types and conditions than any other lures, or, for that matter, any natural bait. Jigs work whether the trout are in deep or shallow water, over sand, shell, or grass bottom. Incidentally, when the flats are cluttered up with floating grass (a fairly common condition in Florida west coast areas) jigs are about the only lures that can be fished without fouling up hopelessly. They sink quickly, avoiding the floating debris long enough to give you at least a partial retrieve. The smaller, lighter spinning jigs respond so well to rod-tip manipulation that you can nearly always coax sea trout to hit them if you experiment long enough. The basic retrieve should be whippy and not too fast, gauged so that the lure will bounce along a sand or shell bottom, or dart just above the grass. Normally, this technique will catch more than its share of trout, but sometimes they demand variations.

Wes Henson and I once had a downright frustrating time trying to hook some unidentified fish that repeatedly nipped at our spinning bucktails. Fishing in a shallow swash channel off the mouth of a creek at Sanibel Island on South Florida's Gulf coast, we discovered after a lot of experimenting that we could get plenty of strikes if we cast across the channel and allowed the tide to roll our lures along the bottom. Trouble was, we just couldn't seem to make permanent contact with the striking fish.

Wes, a sharp ex-catfisherman from the Midwest, finally came up with an idea. When he felt a nipping strike, he lowered his rod tip instead of striking back. I saw his line jerk taut, and he was fast to a fish. A few moments later, Wes slipped the net under a sleek two-pound spotted sea trout.

"For a newcomer to salt-water spinning, you're sure

doing okay," I remarked. "It never occurred to me to delay my strike like that with a deep-fished artificial."

Wes grinned. "Just like drifting bait for channel cats in Stony Creek back in Illinois," he said. "If you strike too soon you miss 'em."

Wes Henson's channel-cat system accounted for a beautiful catch before the tide turned and action ceased, and it certainly pointed up the fact that it pays to experiment and try all sorts of techniques before giving up on sea trout.

When the sea trout are feeding over shallow flats, miniature top water spinning plugs can produce lots of action. The little plunkers, darters, and injured minnows occasionally take trout when the more consistent bucktails fail. Trout like a surface lure, whether fly, spinning, or casting; and they like it fished bass style: slowly, and noisily. They'll usually swirl at it several times before striking, and an increase in retrieve speed will often make a swirling fish latch on. A correspondent of mine, F. L. Mattfeldt of Atlanta, tells me that he's made some great catches of extra-big sea trout in North Florida by fishing a darter persistently around pilings and channel-markers. This makes sense, as big trout very definitely like darters . . . and channel-markers.

There is little doubt that the most generally effective sea trout rig for the bait-casting rod is a surface or underwater plug trailed by a slightly weighted streamer fly or fly-rod jig. The fly is easily attached to the tail hook of the plug by a couple of feet of monofilament nylon. If the trailer fly is not weighted, it will continually foul on the hooks of the plug, so be sure it packs just enough weight to swing it free on the cast. This rig is a real trout killer, the plug attracting them and the trailer clinching the deal. Usually, a noisy surface lure is the best bet for the trailer rig, but sometimes a torpedo style underwater plug works even better. The real originators of this rig were commercial sea trout fishermen, who found that trout could be attracted to their live minnow baits by use of a popping cork. The plug-fly combination is merely a variation of this. Tackle salesman Marty Foster deserves much of the credit for popularizing the trailer fly or jig in Florida, but it was New Jersey's Bill Upperman who gave Marty the idea ... and Bill has sold a lot of his bucktails as a result.

Not long ago I got the notion that spotted sea trout in shallow water might be vulnerable to a bass-style pork chunk fished on a weedless hook. There are times when the trout grub through the ribbon grass in extremely shallow water, and it is difficult to fish a conventional sinking lure for them without hanging it on the grass. Surface lures don't produce very well when the trout are grubbing, because they're look-ing for mollusks and crustaceans hiding under the grass, not for surface food. A weedless hook and pork chunk, I reasoned, would slither through the grass so alluringly that no grubbing trout could resist it.

I carried a supply of weedless hooks and Uncle Josh pork frogs for several fishing trips without finding the trout in a grubbing mood, but finally a friend and I found them in a shallow grass bar in San Carlos Bay. Without comment, I snapped a weedless hook on my leader and opened the jar of Uncle Josh frog chunks.

My companion, who prefers to remain anonymous, thought that the Florida sun had at last caught up with me. "Going to catch a bass?" he asked. "This isn't Lake Okee-chobee, you know."

I held my silence and cast the frog chunk out over the

grass bar, letting it settle into the ribbon grass. Then I began to reel slowly and hesitatingly, making the wiggling pork frog crawl right through the grass. My partner just shook his head and made uncalled-for observations on my sanity.

"Get busy and fish," I snapped. "I'm experimenting."

When I had retrieved the pork chunk some thirty feet I felt a light strike. I twitched the lure. Suddenly a fish latched on, and moments later I popped a nice spotted sea trout into the icebox. Two more casts with the frog chunk put two more trout on ice, but my companion couldn't hook anything but ribbon grass on his jig.

When I hooked the fourth trout my buddy broke down. "Got another one of those rigs?" he asked meekly.

"Going to catch a bass?" I inquired.

"Dammit, Phil, I apologize. Give me a hook and pork chunk, and let's catch some fish," he pleaded.

We proceeded to do just that, hooking and landing trout almost at will until the falling tide became too low and the fish left the shallow flat. With standard bucktail jigs we'd probably have caught a few fish, but not nearly so many as the pork frogs were able to get. Sea trout, of course, couldn't be expected to recognize a real frog if they saw one, but those wiggly pork chunks simply looked good to eat . . . and they didn't hang up on the ribbon grass.

The spotted sea trout is one of the few salt-water fish that readily hits fresh-water-style bass plugs. Most of the standard wigglers and wobblers found in every bass fisherman's tackle box are fairly good trout lures. While these plugs are not so effective as most of the lures designed especially for salt water, they are a pretty good bet for the fresh-water angler who has had no experience at manipulating salt-water-style lures. Jigs, clothespins, and the like must be activated with the rod, while most bass plugs need only to be reeled in. One word of caution: Fit your bass plugs with tinned hooks before getting salt on them. The bronzed or nickel-plated hooks generally supplied won't last long after the salt-water treatment.

When sea trout are feeding over the shallower grass flats, there's a barrel of fun to be had via a fly rod. Popping bugs, feather minnows, streamer flies, and fly-spinner combinations will really make trout forget their table manners. I prefer surface bugs when fly-fishing for sea trout, because I like to see (and hear) them strike. Trout don't seem to be particular about color in cork-bodied bugs, so presumably they figure cork is cork, no matter what color it's painted. Try a wingless popper in size 1 or 1/o, and work it slowly, with loud pops. If the water is shallow and trout are around, you should get action.

Almost any streamer fly will take trout when they're in shallow water—say no deeper than four feet. Patterns like the Micky Finn, Grey Ghost, Light Tiger, and Black Ghost are all good, but it is not at all necessary to use such fancy styles. A bit of yellow or white bucktail tied on a size 2 tinned O'Shaughnessy hook will work just as well as the expensive patterns . . . and the hook won't rust as a standard streamer hook will. Short-shank hooks are better for sea trout streamers than long shanks, as trout practically always take a fly head first. Streamer flies and fly-spinner combinations are most effective when fished in slow jerks just above the grass. Where the water depth is greater than four feet, a spinner fly is more useful than a plain streamer because of its better sinking characteristics.

Best natural baits for sea trout in Florida waters are live

shrimp, live minnows, and cut mullet, in that order. It is best to fish these baits with a float to keep them a foot or so above the grass and out of reach of pinfish, sea catfish, and other bait-stealers. A popping cork is very useful in bait-fishing for trout, attracting them to the bait from a considerable distance. The cork should be popped loudly once or twice, then allowed to rest for a half-minute or so. Popping corks may be obtained from most tackle shops in the coastal areas, or may be made from large bottle corks simply by hollowing out the large end. They are attached and used like a regular bobber, but should pop loudly when jerked on the water.

Bait-fishing for trout is most fun with spinning or light casting tackle. Spinning gear is best for live shrimp or minnows fished without float or weight (a highly effective method, incidentally), while the casting rod is more suitable for use with a popping cork. A hook size of about 1/0 is right for all sea trout bait-fishing, whether a casting rod, spinning rod, or cane pole is used.

If you want to boat a respectable percentage of the spotted sea trout you hook, you'd better use a landing net. Their soft mouth tissue just doesn't permit swinging them in by the line, and their not-so-soft teeth rule out the thumb-in-mouth landing method. Buy a big, aluminum-frame net, and you'll more than pay for it the first time you go sea trout fishing.

Many Florida Gulf coast fishermen consistently pay expenses by selling all or part of their sea trout catches to the skiff liveryman. While it is legal for Florida residents to do this, nonresident anglers must buy a commercial fishing license before they may legally sell their fish.

Perhaps the most appealing characteristics of Florida's

spotted sea trout are his willingness to be caught by any fishing method and his extremely long range over the coastal areas of the state. Whether you are a bait-caster, fly-fisherman, spin-caster, or like to mix brands, you can catch your share of sea trout. If you enjoy still-fishing with a cane pole and live bait, you can use this method and catch sea trout. From Jacksonville to Miami to Pensacola, you'll find them wherever you can find grassy bottom. Keep your tackle light to get the most out of their modest fight. The sea trout, I repeat, is a boxer, not a slugger.

CHAPTER 9

They Call Him Red

FLORIDA's inshore salty waters are the stomping grounds of many of the world's best game fish. In no other area in the United States are so many different species of hard-fighting fish to be found. Many creditable scrappers that receive top billing in other sections of the country would be passed up as mediocre game here. A fish must have plenty on the ball to gain recognition in the fast company of such tackle tormentors as the bonefish, the tarpon, the snook, the barracuda, the lady-fish, and the various members of the jack family. Few fishes common to other areas could make the grade.

There is one, however—one stubborn battler common to the southern half of the Eastern seaboard—that has bulled its way to a highly regarded position among Florida's finny residents. Indeed, this fish is the odds-on favorite of a sizable proportion of the coastal angling fraternity from Jacksonville to Pensacola. Redfish, they call him . . . red, for short. Ichthyologists name him *Sciænops ocellatus*. You may know him as drum, red drum, bar bass, bull bass, or by any one of his fifteen or twenty local aliases. His accepted name is channel bass.

Although the name channel bass is used in check lists of the American Fisheries Society and the Outdoor Writers Association of America, this fish is not a bass at all, but a member of the croaker family. Specifically, the channel bass is a drum, and is known as such throughout much of his range.

A year-round resident of Florida waters, the channel bass seems to be a rugged individualist among the state's fish. When other fish are on a feeding rampage and easy to catch, the channel bass may go on a hunger strike. On the other hand, the channel bass often provides a lot of sport when fishing in general is extremely slow. On many occasions, covering all seasons of the year, reds have come through for me when the fishing situation seemed hopeless.

One beautiful day in February, Johnny Herbert and I found ourselves in the embarrassing position of having to apologize to a Californian for some disgustingly slow Florida fishing. The Californian, John Harmon of Oakland, while disappointed with the fishing, seemed to be enjoying the situation immensely. Each time we moved from one area of San Carlos Bay to another, unsuccessfully attempting to lure some fish with our spinning bucktails, Harmon would drop a remark to the effect that the California Chamber of Commerce would enjoy hearing about this. All Johnny and I could do was brag about the sunny, eighty-degree weather and grope for excuses for the lack of fish.

"The tide's almost high now," I said lamely. "We'll get some fish soon."

Johnny perked up. "Hey," he said, "let's run over to

Matlacha Pass and look for reds around the oyster bars. The tide's getting about right for them."

It was a four-mile run to Matlacha Pass, and when we got there the tide had just turned out. As we approached the first line of oyster bars, Johnny tossed his bucktail up on the shoals and made immediate contact with a heavy fish. After a dogged, head-shaking fight, he led a beautiful eight and one-half-pound channel bass into the net.

Harmon's eyes popped. "Say," he said, "that's a dam' nice fish."

Johnny shrugged. "Run of the mill," he said. "We usually throw this size back."

I eased the boat close to the bar again, made a cast, and I too was immediately involved with a channel bass. Then Johnny got another, and I another, and we caught them alternately until the tide had dropped too far, and the reds left the bars. John Harmon, using a very limber, eight-foot spinning rod, didn't get a fish. His whippy rod simply wouldn't control the lure well enough to allow him to work it across the oyster bottom without hanging up. Nevertheless, Harmon had to admit that Florida fishing was pretty hot stuff . . . thanks to channel bass.

Channel bass have been great favorites of mine ever since my first attempt at salt-water spinning, when I hooked and landed three ten-pounders in successive casts. On that occasion I was with tarpon guide Eddie Fitzpatrick of Fort Myers, trying to get some photographs of Eddie and tarpon in action. The tarpon weren't in the mood to be photographed, however, and just for something to do while waiting for their cooperation I decided to try a few casts with my brand-new spinning outfit. My wrists still ache when I think about how I struggled with those reds, unaccustomed and unconditioned as I was to handling big fish with the new-fangled gear. But they sold me on spinning, and made me respect them highly as game fish. I didn't even care that the tarpon never would consent to having their pictures taken that day.

Every time I hook even a small channel bass on light gear I think of Izaak Walton's expression: "very shie to be landed." He'll allow himself to be led toward the boat or beach, offering only token resistance. Then a wave of bashfulness will come over him and he'll surge into a power-laden run with a suddenness that's likely to catch you with your rod down. This change of pace seems to be cloaked in the indecision of the redfish himself, and it is almost impossible to anticipate his moves. The channel bass is not a champion for top straight-away speed, but his acceleration is exceptional, and he's very fast for a fish of his build. His reserve energy is that of a well-trained athlete. Time after time you think he's whipped, and time after time he breaks into another run. He's a rough-and-tumble, rowdy roughneck—yet a clean fighter willing to slug it out with you in the open rather than to seek obstructions on which to foul your line. This characteristic makes the channel bass in sizes up to ten pounds excellent quarry for the light-tackle enthusiast who likes to cast along mangrove shore lines or oyster bars.

What a rugged digestive system the channel bass has! I doubt that any other fish would be capable of matching his varied diet. His mouth is that of a typical bottom-feeder, and a portion of his fare parallels that of the bottom-feeding fin-sters. Mollusks, shrimp and crabs of all sorts are always pleasing to his taste buds. The fact that these entrees have claws or armor plating doesn't bother him, for his throat is equipped with built-in bone-crushing machinery. When he feels in the mood for a bit of exercise along with his meal, the channel bass enjoys running down any forage fish small enough to swallow. I have seen schools of small channel bass use the wolf-pack tactics of bluefish, herding fingerling mullet into compact groups, then chopping the groups to pieces. The channel bass might well be called omnivorously carnivorous, for he likes any and all sea foods of animal origin.

He will take any and every natural bait or artificial lure normally used in salt-water angling—and many lures not normally used in salt-water angling. I have caught channel bass on every type of artificial lure made except the dry fly. My daughter even caught one on a night crawler, while fishing for bream in a brackish Florida creek! While it is true that channel bass will take just about anything in the way of a bait or lure at one time or another, they do have certain moods and preferences. Judging from the contents of dozens of stomachs I've examined, I'd say without hesitation that their favorite natural foods in Florida waters are crustaceans. Nearly all of them contain crabs of some sort: blue crabs, stone crabs, or mangrove crabs. Shrimp also seem to be an important item in their natural diet, with small fish an occasional rather than a regular entree.

The channel bass ranges in size from less than a pound up to fifty pounds or bigger in Florida, and it is difficult to name a flat average. In general, the biggest specimens are found in the surf and inlets from Melbourne north, and these may average, say, twenty pounds. In South Florida, the size runs considerably smaller, with ten-pounders considered large and twenty-pounders exceptional fish.

Schools of channel bass contain fish of approximately the

same size, with little variation among the individual members. The largest schools are made up of the smallest fish, and the larger the individual fish, the smaller the school. The very largest specimens tend to be solitary in habit except during migratory or spawning runs, while redfish of ten pounds or smaller are nearly always gregarious. While young channel bass do not ordinarily school compactly like bluefish or jacks, it is always safe to assume that where one is caught, others are nearby.

Although I was introduced to channel bass on the beaches of North Carolina, where the fish run extremely large, I must confess that I've had much more fun with them in South Florida, where they are relatively small. The three- to ten-pound redfish of Florida's lower west coast are excellent light-tackle fish, just right for spinning, casting, or fly-fishing.

Although I like the little ones better, I'll always remember the big channel bass I almost caught one day with spinning tackle in San Carlos Bay. I had been plugging the shore line of a small island for snook and had just raised a nice one that rolled at the plug but wouldn't take it. I picked up my spinning outfit, which was rigged with a size 1 Upperman bucktail, hoping to surprise the snook with the different lure. My cast was hardly complete when I felt something heavy slam into the bucktail. The fish made straight for open water and settled down to a deep, jarring, extremely dogged fight. I wrestled with him for nearly a half-hour, not getting a glimpse of him until his spirit broke and he rolled up to the boat exhausted. It was a channel bass, the biggest channel bass I'd seen since the day I beached a thirty-pounder in North Carolina. My landing net looked pitifully small as I tried to jockey that big red into it, and I put it down and groped under the floor boards for the gaff. Suddenly there was a heavy tug at my rod and a great deal of splashing. I looked up to see a shark munching on my prize channel bass! One bite, and I had only the head to show for my half-hour fight. The head, which had been bitten off right at the gills, weighed five pounds!

While light-tackle fishermen in Florida catch significant numbers of channel bass more or less accidentally when fishing for other fish, reds may be taken much more regularly by fishing expressly for them. Redfish stick pretty close to the mangroves or oyster bars along Florida's bays and creeks, and accurate, close-in casting is necessary to get them. Whether you use a fly, casting, or spinning rod, it's a lot of fun trying to put your lure up under the mangroves again and again without hanging up. And it's even more fun when a nice red takes hold.

For bait-casting or spinning, the best lures for channel bass are feather or bucktail jigs in one-eighth- to one-half-ounce sizes and a generous assortment of colors. These fish sometimes get unshakable notions about what they want in the way of lure color, and if you can't show them the hue they happen to be looking for, you just won't do business with them. I have had many experiences to bear this out.

On one occasion, Al Finkelstein of Baltimore and I were fishing for snook with feather jigs on bait-casting tackle in the lower Imperial River. Al was using a yellow jig, while mine had a red head and white tail. Otherwise, the jigs were identical. As we drifted past a small mangrove key near the mouth of the river, Al hooked a fish.

"It doesn't feel like a snook," he remarked. "Must be a jack."

The fish surged from one short run into another, boring

deep and shaking his head. I held the boat clear of the mangroves and watched until Al worked him to the boat. It turned
out to be a channel bass weighing about three pounds.

"Let's anchor here for a while, Al," I said. "Reds usually
run in schools."

After anchoring in a strategic position, we began casting
our jigs alongside the little island. Al immediately hooked another channel bass, an exact duplicate of his first. Then
another, and still another, while I hadn't even had a strike.
Finally, I did get a strike, but it turned out to be a little snook,
not a channel bass. I got an idea.

"Al, this looks like a good time to try an experiment," I
said. "How about swapping lures with me for a few casts?"

Al saw what I was up to and readily agreed. My second
cast with the yellow jig brought me a channel bass, while Al's
casts with the red-and-white lure failed to produce. Then we
both used yellow jigs, and we both caught channel bass. We
switched back to red-and-white jigs for a few casts from time
to time with negative results, but until the school either left or
got wise, we were able to take channel bass on yellow jigs
with no trouble.

That experience certainly proved that channel bass can
be extremely color conscious, for it was the most clear-cut case
of color selectivity in fish I've ever seen. It did not prove that
yellow is always better than red and white for channel bass, so
don't make the mistake of jumping to such a conclusion. I
have caught plenty of channel bass on red-and-white jigs and
bucktails, and I have also seen the time when yellow wouldn't
tempt these fish.

One windy day in March, Manny Eisfeld and I ran our
boat into a large sheltered cove off Matlacha Pass on Pine

Island to see what we could do about getting out of the wind. The mangrove shore line looked pretty fishy, and we elected to concentrate our efforts in these shady, quiet waters. I maneuvered the boat to within an easy cast of the mangroves, then throttled the outboard down and idled along parallel to shore. We began to cast in under the mangroves, using spinning tackle and Number 1 Upperman bucktails, Manny a yellow one and I a blue.

My third or fourth cast brought a heavy strike, and I was fast to a powerful fish. I gunned the motor and pulled out from the shore for fighting room, holding the fish hard against the bend of the rod. I got the jump on him and broke him away from the mangroves before he realized what was happening. When he finally did try to make it back to the roots, I was able to stop his runs short of them. After a tough, dogged fight, I slipped the net under a channel bass in the eight-pound class.

Again we eased along the shore line and cast our bucktails back under the overhanging branches, and again I made contact with a channel bass. This one, too, allowed me to bull him out from the mangrove roots with the outboard motor and wear him down in open water. Another eight-pounder. After landing this fish, I stopped casting for a while to concentrate on handling the boat for Manny, but fifty yards of inviting shore line didn't produce even a strike for him.

"Maybe you got the only fish here," Manny said.

"Maybe," I agreed.

I picked up my rod and made a cast with the blue bucktail, and darned if I didn't snag another channel bass. After landing the fish I dug into my tackle box and found another blue Upperman for Manny. "Try this," I said. "I've seen reds act stubborn about color before."

Sure enough, the blue lure turned the trick, and Manny, too, began to get action with the channel bass. Before they stopped hitting we boated nineteen and lost only one in the mangrove roots . . . all on blue bucktails. Another amazing demonstration of color selectivity in these fish.

(Incidentally, I make my blue bucktails by simply dyeing white ones in ordinary Rit or Tintex. Since these are all-purpose dyes, which work on nylon, rayon and acetate as well as vegetable and animal fibers, they dye the lacquered head and wrap as well as the hair on bucktail jigs. I would never be without a few blue lures when salt-water fishing.)

At times, spoons and small plugs are well received by channel bass, but these lures are far less consistent than jigs. Small surface lures occasionally work wonders, and no fish hits a top water plug with more gusto than a hungry red. He tries to smash it with savage force, probably because his mouth is shaped inefficiently for surface-feeding, and he's afraid it will escape if he doesn't hit it hard. Fly-rod poppers and the little spinning size darters and plunkers are probably the best surface lures for channel bass, but large zaragossa-style plugs often work equally well.

A lure, whether surface or underwater, should be worked slowly for channel bass to give them plenty of time to look it over. This applies to spoons, jigs, plugs, and flies. The slower the retrieve, the better. This does not mean that action should be lacking, however, for reds like action in a lure as well as the next fish. A whipping action of the rod tip will keep the lure alive, even while it is being retrieved very slowly. Remember that channel bass are essentially bottom-feeders, as evidenced by their mouth shape, and bottom-feeders like to grub along and take their time about eating as a general rule.

Tackle for school-size channel bass need not be anything special, ordinary fresh-water gear being just about perfect. Guides, reels, and all hardware must be resistant to salt-water corrosion, of course, but that's about the only basic requirement. Your bass outfit will probably fill the bill. I use five-pound line in spinning for them, ten-pound line for bait-casting, and a leader tapered to six pounds for fly-fishing. Such light gear is adequate. While a wire leader is not absolutely essential for small channel bass, snook are frequently encountered along with them, and it does pay to use from nine to twelve inches of wire just in case.

The really big channel bass that roam the surf and inlets of North Florida's east coast are not exactly made to order for fresh-water tackle, although experienced fishermen take them regularly with bait-casting and spinning gear. These fish sometimes run to forty or fifty pounds, and it takes either authoritative tackle or a high degree of angling skill to cope with their long, surging runs and bulldogging tactics. In the larger inlets, such as the mouth of the St. Johns River, big reds may be taken on big spoons or plugs trolled with thirty-six- to forty-five-pound-test nylon on star drag reels large enough to hold about 200 yards of the line used. Trolling rods of bamboo or glass with six- to nine-ounce tips should complete the tackle.

For channel bass surf-fishing, either a Calcutta pole or a standard surf rod with thirty-inch spring butt and a tip of six or six and one-half feet is rigged with a wide-spool squidding reel full of 200 yards of nine- to twelve-thread linen or its equivalent in nylon. A three- to four-foot stainless steel leader is used on a "fish-finder" rig, with a four-ounce pyramid sinker and a size 8/0 to 10/0 hook. Best bait for the surf is probably a small live blue crab, but mossbunker or cut mullet will prove successful baits when blue crabs are not available.

Channel bass are most likely to be found in the North Florida surf on the incoming tides, when they seek food right in the breakers. The most productive technique in surf-casting is to drop the bait just beyond the breakers and then move it in a few feet at a time, with pauses of several minutes between moves. The strike will generally begin as a sly tug. When this occurs, throw the reel into free spool and bide your time. Old Red will probably mouth the bait for a while before grabbing it for keeps, and the fish-finder rig mentioned above allows the line to run freely through the eye of the sinker so he won't feel the weight and get wise. When the line starts out fast, throw the reel in gear and sock him hard.

No Florida fish is more versatile than the channel bass from the standpoint of variety of angling methods applicable to his capture. Feeding in all water levels from top to bottom and eating nearly anything, he can be caught with just about any tackle you care to use. You'll meet him in the surf, in inlets and passes, up rivers, and around shallow bars in bays. Select an outfit suitable for the water you're fishing, and you've usually got the right style and weight tackle for Red. Whether you take him by trolling, surf-casting, bait-casting, fly-fishing, spinning, or with nothing but a hand line, you'll find him a game fish capable of holding his own in any company.

In sizes up to ten pounds, the channel bass makes fine eating. The flesh is firm, white, and clean-tasting. He is one of the most popular food fishes in Florida, but is not so highly regarded in some other areas. Perhaps they don't prepare him right elsewhere. Try him skinned, and filleted, and fried to a golden brown in deep fat. There's a dish to make any lover of sea food drool! The larger channel bass are supposed to be too coarse for table use, but who wants to eat a big one anyway? Who could?

CHAPTER 10

The Misunderstood Barracuda

Long before I ever caught—or even saw—a barracuda, I had acquired some pretty silly ideas about his game qualities . . . or lack of them. Most of the books I had read wrote him off as a nuisance fish, not worth the bait needed to catch him. One well-known angling authority conceded that the barracuda would strike hard and start fast, but said he would "quit cold" when stopped.

So I thought I knew all about 'cudas when I got my first chance to do some fishing for them, and I felt that I could handle the biggest of them with a light bait-casting outfit and ten-pound-test line. My partner and guide on that first barracuda trip suggested that I'd better use one of his star drag reels unless I had a thumbstall (which I hadn't), but I figured he was just making with typical guide talk. We ran out to Alligator Lighthouse, about three miles off Islamorada, hooked on small mullet strips, and went to trolling. We hadn't trolled far when I almost lost my rod to the doggonedest strike I'd ever felt. Seconds later my left thumb was bleeding, and my right forefinger seemed to be out of joint where the reel handles had clobbered it. But I managed to exert some pressure and stop the fish. I stopped him long enough to see him jump twice, then laid the rod on him to pump him in. But the fish had other ideas, and he proceeded to run more, and to jump more, and to fight as long as any other fish of comparable size I'd ever caught on casting tackle. Yes, it was a barracuda, a mere five-pound barracuda that didn't know he was supposed to quit cold when stopped.

I don't know where or how the "experts" who ridicule the barracuda as a fighter get their information, but it obviously can't be from personal experience with 'cudas on sporting tackle. Maybe they catch all their five- and six-pounders on tuna tackle, or perhaps they get them to quit cold with dynamite. Every barracuda I've caught—and I've landed hundreds —has fought the same furious fight put up by my first one, and the only times they've quit cold were when other 'cudas cut 'em off behind the gills. Even then, they'd wiggle whatever they had left and try to continue the scrap.

The great barracuda is unquestionably one of the finest light-tackle fish in existence anywhere, a fighting fish without a serious weakness. His so-so reputation in some quarters results from his being hooked too often on tackle designed for much heavier game. For a great many years it was practically unheard of to fish purposely for barracuda, and most of them were caught along the outer reefs on the edge of the Gulf Stream by anglers seeking bigger and more exotic game. Nowadays the barracuda is probably the most popular game fish in the Florida Keys . . . and that's saying something, for Keys waters are loaded with some pretty hot game fish.

The barracuda is very plentiful from Miami southward through the Keys. During the summer months he migrates northward up the Atlantic coast, becoming fairly plentiful as far north as Fort Pierce and Vero Beach. The fishing pressure on him is tremendous, but he doesn't seem to mind. As fast as 'cudas are caught from any given spot, others move in to take their place. Day after day, the same stretches of shore line, the same reef patches, and the same banks yield barracudas in seemingly inexhaustible supply. Sport fishing can't hurt the 'cuda population, because these fish eat each other at a much faster rate than they can be caught by sporting methods. And since 'cudas are not netted commercially in Florida, the outlook for future barracuda fishing is very bright.

The barracuda is popularly supposed to be a savage, incautious sea tiger that strikes viciously at anything moving in the water, but this is just another of the many misconceptions about him. Actually, the barracuda is an even-tempered, easygoing fish, neither given to reckless and gluttonous feeding nor susceptible to teasing. Barracudas don't hunt in packs, nor do they kill other fish for the mere sake of killing, like bluefish. They do not fly off the handle and strike lures out of sheer cussedness, as bass and some other fish are apt to do. The only way you can get a barracuda to strike a lure is to convince him that it is good eating and that there are no strings attached . . . and he's hard to convince. Small barracudas, youthfully naive, are ready strikers, but as they grow up they become more and more cautious.

I know of no fish harder to fool with artificial lures than adult barracudas. Their ability to detect a phoney is particularly impressive when you consider their hearty appetites, curious nature, and lack of fear. 'Cudas don't run from your boat, and they don't shy away from your lures; they follow at a safe distance, curiously, but steadfastly refuse to strike if the lure doesn't suit them. If the adjective "smart" can be applied to any fish, then the barracuda is smart, second only to the mangrove snapper as the smartest fish I've ever encountered. This may come as a surprise to you, but it's true, nevertheless.

About the only way to fool *big* barracuda is to catch them off guard. I was anchored over a little reef patch off Key Largo one morning, having myself a whale of a time catching baby amberjacks with weighted bucktails on a long, extra-light spinning rod and four-pound-test line. One of the little jacks I hooked seemed especially wild, and the reason soon became apparent. A large 'cuda, about a four-footer, had appeared on the scene. There was a sudden swirl, a sharp jolt on my rod, then my line went slack and I reeled in part of the head of the little amberjack. The big barracuda had snipped him off just behind the hook, and was lying in wait right beside the boat for a whack at another one. Unhooking the jack head, I tossed it overboard, and the 'cuda practically caught it as it hit the water. Then I flipped in my little buck-tail, and the 'cuda caught it too! I caught him off guard, all right, but I was off guard myself, as I could have picked up one of my heavier spinning outfits instead of using the light one. As it turned out, the 'cuda showed no sign of tiring after twenty-five minutes, finally breaking the four-pound line by running fast through some floating seaweed with it.

Practically all big barracudas caught on artificial lures are hooked in such unguarded moments as the one described above. I've hooked them by spotting them first, then placing a cast so that the lure could be skittered just behind them. Frequently this technique causes them to turn like a flash and grab it. Success with big 'cudas on artificials lies in not giving them a good look at the lure, for once they've had a chance to peg it as a phoney you can't make 'em hit, no matter how hard you try. There are exceptions, of course, but don't count on them.

During the special fishing tournament conducted for the Outdoor Writers Association of America meeting in Miami in 1952, I met such an exceptional barracuda. Under the iron structure of a blinker-type channel-marker off Key Largo I spotted a group of king-size 'cudas . . . really big ones, from about twenty to forty pounds. I circled the blinker once to lure them out, and out they came, filing in behind the boat like sheep. Cutting the motor, I began casting my spinning bucktail at them, telling myself that I was about to come up with a winning entry in the spinning division of the writer's tourney. Several dozen casts without so much as a close follow, however, had me telling myself another story, something to the effect that I didn't really care about winning anything in the tournament anyway. As a final resort I decided to try bouncing the bucktail on the sandy bottom with a slow re-trieve, but I didn't really expect it to work in twelve feet of water with the fish lying just under the surface. Yet it did work, and I found myself in combat with about twenty-five pounds of angry 'cuda. The fight was fast and furious for a while, runs and jumps coming in rapid succession, but the fish soon decided he'd better pace himself. As he slowed down to a dogged tug of war, I noticed that an even bigger 'cuda was following him. Suddenly a terrific jolt shook my rod, and the water in the vicinity of the hooked fish exploded. A five-footer had taken my four-footer, cutting or breaking the five-pound line in the process! And although there were still a couple of dozen big 'cudas around, not another one would fall for the bottom-bounced bucktail. The single frivolous one was decapitated for his mistake! Incidentally, that same blinker has since yielded me many nice barracuda. It's Blinker BH31, best reached from Gulfstream Fishing Lodge or Reilly's Beachhead, on upper Key Largo, in case you're interested.

For fast and furious barracuda fishing, the little ones are your best bet. There are thousands upon thousands of little 'cudas from eight to thirty inches long in the shallows inshore and offshore on the Florida Keys. They are so numerous that Mother Nature just had to provide a way to thin their ranks, for if they all grew up the ocean wouldn't be big enough to feed them. Mother Nature's gimmick was simple: she made 'em reckless. Young 'cudas are the perfect antithesis of old ones; the little ones are as stupid as the big ones are smart. They'll keep hitting a lure until hooked, then come back and hit it again if they happen to get away the first time. But they fight hard and fast, and make for a barrel of fun with light tackle. The lightest of spinning gear is ideal for small 'cudas, with bucktails like the size 1 Upperman the best lures. They'll chop the hair off bucktails, eat the nylon windings, and fill the lead head with tooth marks, but as long as they leave you something to cast, they'll continue to hit it if you continue to cast it.

The best natural bait for barracudas of any size is fresh mullet, preferably in strips from four to six inches long. Mullet strips may be trolled with any tackle you care to use, or may be cast and retrieved like an artificial lure. Far more effective than casting strip baits, however, is trolling them at slow to moderate speed. Barracudas are so curious that they cannot resist following a moving boat, just to look it over, and as they fall in behind the boat they get a look at the trolled strip. This is a good thing to know when you're after 'cudas, for you can actually "chum" them up by running your boat in a circle over 'cuda water . . . even without trolling anything. One circle over a shallow reef will nearly always bring several barracudas into casting range. Indeed, barracudas are so fond of following boats that you'll get two or three times as many by casting behind a drifting boat as you will by trying to fish the undisturbed water ahead of the boat. Curiosity has killed far more 'cudas than cats.

The barracuda's curious nature is probably at least partly responsible for his reputation as a threat to human life. He does seem to find human swimmers or waders intensely fascinating, and it takes a steel-nerved stoic to meet a big 'cuda face to face in the water without getting panicky. If you retreat from a 'cuda, either by swimming or wading, he'll follow, but not with any idea of attacking. He just can't figure you out, yet his curiosity compels him to try. If you move slowly toward a 'cuda, he'll back off and keep his distance; if you make a quick move in his direction, he'll scram.

Many thousands of man-hours are spent annually by goggle fishermen over barracuda-infested Florida reefs, yet at this writing there has been no record of anyone's being bitten. In fact, the goggle and Aqualung boys depend on barracudas as watchdogs for shark protection when working the outer reefs. The spearfishermen know that no dangerous sharks are around as long as the 'cudas swim along and watch them fish, but when the 'cudas vanish, "It's time to get the hell out of the water," as one spearfisherman put it. The 'cudas sense the approach of sharks very quickly, and the spearfisherman who keeps one eye on his 'cuda contingent always has plenty of time to get in the boat before the sharks arrive on the scene.

The great barracuda is a light-tackle fish, coming in a wide range of sizes to suit all degrees of tackle lightness. For the big 'cudas that prowl the outer reefs on the edge of the Gulf Stream, standard trolling gear with six-ounce tip and nine-thread (twenty-seven-pound) line is in order. The barracudas of the outer reefs run up to forty or more pounds, and they'll work a 6/9 outfit for all it's worth.

For the inner reefs and banks, where the fish average five pounds or less, spinning or casting tackle is ideal. For spinning, use six-pound test monofilament, a rod with a fast tip and reinforced butt, and a sturdy, corrosion-proof reel with a smooth drag. Spinning gear has proven itself amazingly effective on barracuda. You can't beat jigs and bucktails for 'cuda lures, and as previously stated, strips of mullet or other fish make the best natural bait. Sometimes a rapidly worked surface plug does a good job on barracuda, especially in inshore waters near the mangroves.

For casting, a five- or five-and-a-half-foot hollow glass rod and a level-wind reel full of fifteen-pound-test nylon is just about perfect. Don't fail to use a thumbstall—the knitted type that fits over the thumb is best—if you have any regard at all for your thumbs. The same lures as used for spinning, in heavier sizes, are also best for bait-casting. Needless to say, a wire leader is an absolute must for all barracuda fishing. It needn't be more than a foot long.

Fly-fishing for barracuda is feasible but somewhat less practical than either spinning or bait-casting. The fast retrieve 'cudas like is hard to execute with a fly outfit. Streamer flies and small popping bugs or feather minnows are at their best along the shore lines in late evening, when the water is calm and small 'cudas are on the prowl. I have had a lot of fun with a fly rod on the ocean side of Key Largo, catching little barracudas on ordinary bass bugs equipped with a short light-wire trace. The bugs should be worked very rapidly for best results. Streamer flies and fly-rod bugs won't last long when 'cudas begin chewing on them, so it's best to use old ones that you consider expendable.

Barracuda fishing is good the year round in the Florida Keys, with extra-hot fishing periods for big ones during the spring and fall spawning periods. In midsummer, the offshore waters of the Gulf of Mexico produce 'cudas in moderate numbers but very large size. Late summer finds plenty of barracudas along the middle Florida east coast, and here, too, the size may run large.

In the neighborhood of Elbow Reef, off Key Largo, there lives a gigantic specimen of great barracuda, an old, battle-scarred fellow affectionately known as "The Crocodile." I first saw him in the summer of 1954 while fishing over the sand-bottomed potholes in the outer reef. I had chummed up a sizable number of jacks and other reef fish and was busily fighting them, one by one, with my light spinning gear. Without warning, the fish all vanished, losing interest in my bucktail and the fresh mullet chum I hastened to throw out. Then I saw him, a truly awesome barracuda at least six and possibly seven feet long, cruising in slow circles a few feet beneath my boat. After a few minutes, he went away, but I never could get the fish chummed up again that day in that area. Later I learned from Jack Reilly at Gulfstream Fishing Lodge that I had been privileged to gaze upon "The Croc," unchallenged boss of the Elbow Reef fish population. Reilly estimates the Croc's weight at sixty-five to seventy pounds. Many spear-fishermen have met him, but he's too smart to let them get close enough for a shot. Constantly patrolling the deep reefs just inside the Gulf Stream, the Croc occasionally attacks a sailfish hooked by charter boats working the area, but he evidently prefers to steer clear of swimming human beings.

Imaginative writers and gullible readers have given the great barracuda his reputation as a man-killer; but in Florida waters, at least, this reputation is undeserved. People have been bitten by barracudas while removing hooks from their mouths, but that's about the only way. I have questioned native guides and fishermen from Key Largo to Marathon, but have yet to find anyone who knows of an authentic attack on a human being by a barracuda. As one old-timer put it, "Most people seem to think it's more exciting to be bitten by a 'cuda than a shark, and as a result lots of shark attacks get chalked up as 'cuda attacks." In other words, unless the attacker is actually identified by either the victim or witnesses, everyone concerned automatically puts the blame on a barracuda. Perhaps there have been actual attacks by barracudas on human swimmers in Florida waters, but they are so rare that they must be considered freak accidents, ranked categorically with lightning's striking from a cloudless sky and hitting someone. I know a fellow who was actually attacked by a wild cottontail rabbit (no kidding), but I certainly don't feel that this makes rabbits dangerous animals!

It's a good thing the great barracuda doesn't live up to his reputation, because if he really wanted to invade the bathing beaches with the idea of biting human beings, he could do an efficient job of it. The 'cuda's jaws are so powerful, and his teeth so sharp and efficient, that he is capable of chopping fish nearly his own size in two with a single stroke. He cuts clean, right through flesh and bone, without tearing the flesh or leaving a ragged edge. His highly developed choppers make it possible for the barracuda to eat fish that would be too big for him to swallow whole, or to bite off as much as he needs to satisfy his immediate appetite. Small wonder the barracuda has fired the imaginations of writers and armchair adventurers alike!

Forget all the lurid tales you've heard of the bloodthirsty barracuda, and think of him only as a great game fish, for a great game fish he is.

CHAPTER 11

Fun to Catch and Fun to Eat

SOME fish are fighting fools on a line, but not worth the
salt needed to season them in the pan. Others aren't much
as fighters, but are nevertheless worthwhile because of their
excellent eating qualities. But whether you like to catch fish,
or eat them, or both, you'll never find a more desirable trio
than the pompano, the bluefish, and the Spanish mackerel.

Many Florida fishermen—including plenty who spend a
lot of time on pompano water—have the notion that pompano
cannot be caught on hook and line. Since the great majority of
salt-water fishermen have never hooked a pompano, this is
not at all surprising. Pompano, nevertheless, are striking fish,
and they're not so difficult to catch if you go about it right.
For consistent success at pompano fishing, specialized techniques and kid-glove tactics are necessary.

The pompano is one of the few prissy members of the
rough-and-ready jack family. While most of his cousins are

gullible, audacious, and not at all discreet about what they hit or how hard they hit it, the pompano is a highly nervous physical coward, with dainty table manners and a suspicious nature. On a hook, however, he'll fight as hard as any of his jack cousins of the same size . . . and that's saying something, for the jacks are indeed tough cookies.

Once in a while you'll find pompano in a relatively incautious mood, and when you do, you're in for some gruelling fishing. One hot day in 1953 Manny Eisfeld and I got into them off Sanibel Island, where San Carlos Bay meets the Gulf of Mexico. There is a wide, flat delta here, with water from three to six feet deep and a swift tide. The pompano—big ones —were over the delta, and evidently on the feed.

Manny hung Number One, and the way that fish took off you'd have thought he was in the fifteen- or twenty-pound class. The pomp hit near the boat and immediately slanted into a sustained run that buzzed nearly a hundred yards of line from Manny's spinning reel. Manny pumped him back almost to the boat, and again he zipped into a frenzied run. One run followed another, each shorter but not much slower than the preceding one. Manny was sweating plenty when I finally slipped the net under about three dollars and fifty cents' worth of pompano . . . a three-pounder.

We continued drifting with the tide and casting our number 1 bucktails ahead of the boat, bouncing the lures on the bottom with an up-and-down motion. The pompano loved it. Before they stopped hitting, we were actually physically tired from fighting them. Never before or since have I found them so gullible.

The pompano is normally as wary as any fish that swims —much warier than most of them. The fabled bonefish, for example, is a blundering fool compared to him, and so is the wisest old Northern brown trout. At times it is almost impossible even to approach within casting range of a pompano, let alone fool him into taking a lure.

Just a couple of days after Manny and I had found the pompano so receptive at Sanibel, I took Bud Hundertmark over to have a go at them. Bud wasn't too sure he could get them to hit his casting-size jigs, as he had previously seen them caught spinning when they wouldn't go for casting stuff.

"Bud," I said, "these pomps are as eager as aquarium fish at feeding time. They'll hit anything."

We wasted no time loading the boat and running out to the delta. I shut off the motor while we were still over deep water, to let the tide carry us to the shallow feeding grounds —a routine precaution against flushing scary fish.

"Cast ahead of the boat, Bud," I instructed, "and bounce your feather on the bottom as you bring it in."

Bud flipped out a cast, and as his jig struck the water a big pompano frantically skipped out from under it.

"Scary!" Bud exclaimed.

"You landed too close and startled him," I commented.

As Bud started his retrieve, however, two more pompano skittered away in panic. "They're scared of my feather," said Bud. "Try your bucktail."

My one-eighth-ounce bucktail made only a faint "plip" as it landed in the water, but darned if it didn't flush a pompano. A ladyfish hit when I started working the lure, and this commotion sent several more pomps into hysterical, jumping flight.

"No telling how many we're scaring, Bud. When one skips, there are probably a dozen others flushing too. Let's try dragging our lures well behind the boat, to get away from the noise of casting."

We tried it. Behind the free-drifting boat we dragged bucktails and feathers all over the delta, and all over the delta we skipped pompano. We tried anchoring and using all sorts of caution against making noise, even speaking in whispers and remaining as motionless as cigar-store Indians. We cast out with the tide and allowed our lures to rest for several minutes before moving them, but we still skipped pompano. Finally, we did what intelligent fishermen should do under such circumstances; we left the delta and went after spotted sea trout on the grass flats of San Carlos Bay.

These two experiences serve to illustrate that pompano are much like other fish, in that you never can tell just what they're going to do. The mood Bud and I found them in was closer to "normal" than the comparative recklessness they displayed for Manny and me, but a soft approach will usually make for at least some action. Always assume that pompano are in a skittish and suspicious humor, and you'll get 'em fairly consistently.

The classic method of pompano fishing on the Florida "Gold Coast" is surf casting, using the "crossed bait trails" technique. The bait is a sand flea, a flea-shaped crustacean about an inch long, which is easily found and caught as it burrows into the wet beach sand behind each receding wave. Standard surf tackle is used, with a pyramid sinker and a number 1 or 1/o hook on a nylon leader. The fisherman makes one cast at an angle to the beach, then retrieves slowly so that the sinker leaves a trail on the bottom. Then he walks a few paces up the beach and makes another cast across the trail made by his first retrieve, again reeling in slowly to form another sinker trail—which makes an X with the first one. Now the caster takes a position midway between the spots from which his X-forming casts were made and attempts to put his bait right in the junction of the two sinker trails. Then he awaits developments. The theory behind this elaborate technique is that the pompano has an acute sense of smell, and if he comes upon one of the sinker trails, he'll follow it right to the sand flea. Seems far-fetched, but it works. Surf fishermen on Florida's lower east coast use this technique almost exclusively, and they sure get their share of pompano. Live shrimp or clam baits will work nearly as well as sand fleas for pompano in the surf.

Probably the best-known and most commonly used method of artificial-lure fishing for pompano is jigging. The lure is a small feather or bucktail jig, either white or yellow, about two and one-half inches long. Rigged on a casting outfit, the jig is simply tossed off a boat, bridge or sea wall, and allowed to settle to bottom. At regular intervals, the rod tip is raised and lowered sharply, causing the lure to jump from the bottom and settle back down. No retrieve is made until the fisherman is ready to give up and try another spot. An adaptation of the straight up-and-down jigging method involves casting the jig out, allowing it to sink to the bottom, then retrieving by whipping the rod. The reel is used only to take up the slack line caused by the whip of the rod, and the retrieve is prolonged by pauses of several seconds between rod whips.

Jigging, as you might expect, is highly effective with spinning gear. Spinning-size bucktails like the number 1 Upperman, used on light monofilament line, are, in fact, the most successful of all pompano lures. Before spinning became popular in Florida, a catch of three or four pompano in a day's fishing with artificial lures was considered an outstanding angling achievement. Spin-casters, however, think nothing of boating a dozen or two pomps in an afternoon when conditions are right.

While pompano will occasionally strike small plugs and spoons, these lures are not in the same league with jigs or weighted bucktails. A lure favored by some pompano specialists is a small Panama roller shell rigged with a swivel in front and a treble hook behind, the hook and swivel connected by a piece of wire running right through the shell. Cement or solder is poured into the shell to add weight, and the lure is fished by jigging. These shell lures are available in many Florida tackle stores.

Pompano feed mostly on crustaceans and mollusks, showing a special liking for sand fleas, shrimps, and the tiny clams known as coquinas. At times they feed actively on minnows, but not when they can find their favored shellfish. They are said occasionally to "tail," much like bonefish, as they grub in the sand and mud for food, but I have never seen this.

Pompano range from North Carolina south to the Florida Keys, and along the Gulf coast from Florida to Texas. There is a pronounced migration up the east coast beginning in late winter and early spring, and a like migration on the Gulf coast that brings the pompano to Louisiana and Texas in late spring and early summer. Though year-round residents of South Florida waters, pompano are most active and easiest to catch during their migrations. Specifically, the best times for pompano are late winter through spring on the lower east coast of Florida, from spring to midsummer on the upper east coast, and from spring until fall on the Gulf coast.

Look for pompano just inside inlets and passes on the in-coming tide, and just outside of these cuts on the outgoing tide. They will usually be found in water from five to ten feet deep, and when they're on the feed they will generally be within one hundred yards of shore. When the surf is running heavy, pompano will come right into the breakers in search of sand fleas and coquinas, but in calm weather they stick to deeper waters.

Pompano fishing is a highly specialized branch of angling, but not so highly specialized that the average fisherman must forego a fling at it. The specialty part is involved with the lures and tactics used, and just about any type tackle may be adapted to an effective method, lure or bait. For all his dollar- to dollar-and-a-half a pound retail price, the pompano is a fairly plenti-ful fish and within the reach of every angler's pocketbook.

When you get that pompano to the kitchen, here's what to do: Starting at the nose, just above the eyes, cut straight back to the gill cover, leaving the top of the head. Follow the line of the gill cavity to remove the gills and the lower part of the head. Scale him and remove the innards in the regular manner. Now get the broiler hot (an oven setting of 450° or so is about right), sprinkle Mr. Pomp with salt and pepper, baste him with lemon butter, and broil him about five minutes per pound on each side. Now you're ready to learn why the pompous pompano brings over a buck a pound in your local fish market. Worth it, too, don't you think?

Second only to the pompano as an "eatin'" fish, and second to none as a scrapper, is the bluefish. Bluefish are as reckless as pompano are cautious; slashing, devil-may-care strikers and gluttonous feeders. Often travelling in compact schools, they use wolf-pack tactics to annihilate the luckless schools of mullet, menhaden or sardines that happen to get in their way. Vicious, bloodthirsty fish, they are well-muscled, spirited fighters on anybody's fishing line.

In Florida waters, bluefish average somewhat smaller than they do in the North, although occasional giant specimens are landed every year in the Lake Worth and Indian River areas. Most of the blues caught in Florida are mere two- or three-pounders, with the average closer to two than three.

Bluefish runs are fairly well defined along Florida's east coast; they can always be counted upon to show up in the surf and inlets with the first northeaster in September. They sometimes arrive in August, as they did, spottily, in 1954. The first run may be heavy, but the fish do not seem to hang around long after the northeast blow is over. Later runs, in October and November, bring the blues that stay around in the bays and surf until spring. A few stay in such waters as Biscayne Bay and Lake Worth the year round.

You never know when you'll run into bluefish on the west coast of Florida, but they seem to be most plentiful in spring, late summer, and early fall. In the spring of 1954 there was an amazingly large and long-lasting run of blues extending from Tampa Bay down into the Ten Thousand Islands. Ranging in weight from one to three pounds, these fish gave Florida west coast anglers fantastic sport for several weeks. Some years, however, there is no pronounced spring run on the west coast, just the few stragglers that are caught throughout the year in these waters.

Since bluefish run of modest size in Florida, the best way to enjoy catching them is to use the lightest of tackle. Spinning or bait-casting gear as used in fresh water will give mere two- and three-pound blues a chance to really show you what they can do. A few weeks before the large run of bluefish mentioned above, L. A. MacDonald of Dayton, Ohio, joined Wes Henson and me on a one-day trip in the Ten Thousand Islands out of Everglades City. We caught a nice assortment of fish with spinning tackle, including snook, sea trout, redfish and ladyfish, and MacDonald got quite a bang out of it. Just before it was time to start a seven-mile run back to the dock, we made a drift through a natural channel off Indian Key, one of the outer islands, and picked up a few sea trout and crevalle jacks. Then I got the hardest strike of the day, and my little spinning reel squealed as the fish steamed off in a vicious run. Mac and Wes stopped fishing to watch, convinced that I had hooked a really big fish. Several times I worked the fish close to the boat, only to see him zoom off again on another run. It was a solid-feeling fish, all right. When at last he gave up, we were amazed to see that it wasn't a big fish after all, just a Florida-size blue-fish, which later weighed in at two pounds, fourteen ounces.

As we drove home that night, MacDonald thanked us for the fishing trip and commented that he'd have plenty to tell the boys when he got back to Ohio. "But boy," he said, "I'd sure like to have got hold of one of those bluefish!"

Blues certainly give a good account of themselves on light gear, but even in Florida, the light-tackle capital of the world, most of them are caught on tackle meant for much heavier game. This is mainly because the bulk of the blue-fishing in Florida is done in the surf of the east coast, during windy weather, and relatively heavy surf gear is needed to cast a lure out where they are feeding. When fishing from a boat, or anywhere that excessively long casts are not necessary, bluefish should be sought with fresh-water-style tackle.

Blues will hit practically anything in the way of casting

or spinning lures, from fast-sinking jigs to high-floating plugs. I have caught them on bucktail jigs at the rate of about ten to one over all other lures, but this is simply because I am an inveterate user of bucktail jigs in salt water. Feather and nylon jigs are also good, as are spoons, squids, and zaragossa-style plugs. A block tin squid tipped with a short strip of pork rind is hard to beat when the blues are off the beaches and long casts into the wind are necessary to reach them.

Bluefish generally like the moderately fast, whippy retrieve favored by so many of Florida's salt-water fish. They are susceptible to trolling, and this is a good way to locate them just inside or just outside inlets and passes. Actually, the problem in Florida is not one of how to fish for blues; it is a matter of being at the right place at the right time. If you happen to hit them during a run, you'll probably catch a boatload by practically any fishing method you care to use. Otherwise, the blues you catch in Florida will be stragglers that horn in when you're fishing for other fish. Just don't forget to use a wire leader whenever you decide to toss lures around in Florida's salty waters. Bluefish are another of the many sharp-toothed species you're liable to run into.

Not long after I moved to Florida, I heard that a good run of Spanish mackerel was in progress at the municipal fishing pier in Naples. Naturally, there was nothing to do but investigate, so bright and early on a Sunday morning I arrived at the Naples pier. Fishermen lined the railings almost shoulder to shoulder, some of them casting small spoons, others fishing with live minnows on cane poles, and all catching mackerel. I noticed that the rig the bait-casters were using was similar to the one I had often used for shad in Maryland's Susquehanna River: a fly-rod-size spoon with a clincher sinker a couple of

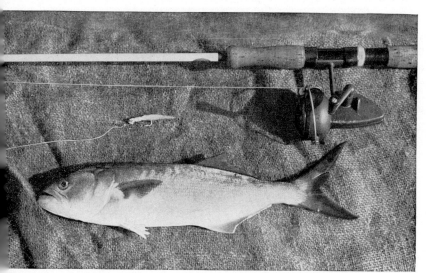

his bluefish is about average size for Florida, around two pounds. Blues are hard
beat, either on a line or in the pan.

gourmet's delight, a two-pound pompano, was caught in Biscayne Bay just
ort cast from downtown Miami. The outsize landing net is a useful piece of
ɔment for the salt-water spin-caster in Florida, for sometimes the fish run big.

9

Dolphin are one of the finest light-tackle fish in existence, made to order for spinning tackle. These were taken by the author about ten miles off Key Largo on the tackle shown—out of a fourteen-foot skiff.

This is Elbow Reef marker, off Key Largo. In the background is a ship running inside the edge of the Gulf Stream.

Ten and three-quarters pounds of little tuna landed by the author in the Gulf Stream off Key Largo on spinning tackle.

For the most fun in Gulf Stream spinning, use an outboard powered skiff, but watch the weather. Here, C. J. Nielsen battles a bonito off Palm Beach, where the Stream runs within a couple of miles of shore.

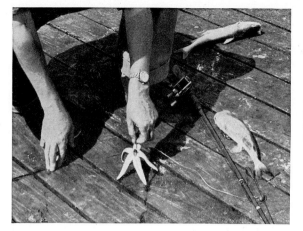

When you drop a bait off a Florida bridge or pier, anything can happen. Here, a perplexed angler caught a starfish! The two conventional fish are sea cats.

A live shrimp is probably the best natural bait you can get for most Florida salt-water fish.

Pier and bridge fishing is great for relaxation, and a great way to soak up wonderful Florida sunshine. This is the municipal fishing pier at Naples.

feet up the line for casting weight. The only difference was that at Naples a wire rather than a nylon leader separated the spoon and sinker, as protection against the mackerel's teeth.

I lost no time in rigging up a small spoon and sinker, and soon I too was catching Spanish mackerel. They were small fish, averaging scarcely a pound, but they'd hit that spoon like a ton of bricks and fight very gamely for their size. Every now and then one would hit the sinker instead of the spoon, and after losing a couple of rigs I learned to attach the clincher to the braided wire leader rather than to the line above it. When they hit a sinker that was fastened to the line, their teeth would cut the line off in the process!

Since that first experience with Spanish mackerel, I've had a chance to do a lot of experimenting with them, but I still haven't found a rig that works better, day in, day out, than the fly-rod spoon and sinker. Mackerel really go for a small spoon fished with a speedy retrieve! White bucktail or nylon jigs are almost as effective, as are small block tin squids . . . but when these lures fail, it's time to snap on a spoon. Sometimes, however, even spoons won't work, and such a situation calls for a little experimenting before throwing in the sponge.

Johnny Herbert and I once found a small school of large Spanish mackerel in Pine Island Sound, jumping like dolphin as they fed on a panicky bunch of small thread herring. Confidently we closed into casting range and worked our white bucktails among the feeding fish, but our confidence dropped a notch or two when our bucktails were ignored. Quickly we dug into our tackle boxes and hauled out shiny new spoons, but a few casts with these made it clear that the mackerel were not interested. Next I tried a little torpedo-shaped top water spinning plug, one from which I had previously removed the spinners to change its action. Casting the plug in the path of a jumping mackerel, I started a fast, skittering retrieve the instant it struck the water. I didn't keep it skittering long, however, for a four-pound Spanish mackerel hit it hard. Johnny snapped on a similar plug with its original equipment of fore-and-aft spinners, but he could not make it skitter properly, and the mackerel wouldn't touch it. When my plug took another fish, Johnny removed the spinners from his, and from there on we had a whale of a time with as nice a bunch of Spanish mackerel as I've ever run across. All we had to do was make our lures act like the skipping and skittering thread herring on which the mackerel were feeding, and they'd hit without hesitation.

Spanish mackerel are found over the entire Florida coast, seasonally in some areas, and on a year-round basis in others. There are always at least a few mackerel along the beaches of South Florida, but these fish are absent during the winter in the northernmost parts of the state. There are large migratory runs down the coasts in fall and northward in spring, providing fast and furious action for all who care to get in on it.

Best fishing places for Spanish mackerel are inlets and passes, the open waters of the larger bays, and the ocean and Gulf beaches from one hundred yards to a half mile offshore. Mackerel are constantly on the move, but the schools tend to hover and circle about buoys, channel-markers, or any school of bait they happen to run across. They are best located by trolling a small spoon or white bucktail over likely water, running the boat in a wide circle rather than shuttling back and forth. While incoming tide is supposed to be best for Spanish mackerel, I have had equally good luck with them during a strong ebb. The best thing to do with Spanish mackerel is take them where and when you find them.

The Spanish mackerel compares favorably with just about any other fish in his weight class in both gameness and edibility. He is strictly light-tackle size, yet is probably taken in greater numbers by trollers using tackle designed for much bigger fish. This is a shame, for the trollers don't know what they're missing. Spinning or light casting tackle and Spanish mackerel complement each other perfectly.

Though they are said to reach a weight of twenty pounds, a Spanish mackerel weighing six should be considered a whopper. A four-pounder is a nice fish, while the average would probably run under two pounds. Most of the outsized specimens of Spanish mackerel reported from time to time are actually cero mackerel, a closely related tropical species seldom found north of the Florida Keys.

C. J. Nielsen and I once got into a curiously mixed bunch of fish off Sanibel Island in the month of August, finding blues, Spanish mackerel, and pompano all feeding together and trying to beat each other to our spinning bucktails. Using two lures at a time, we managed to land some crazy, mixed-up double-headers, and we wound up taking home as beautiful an assortment of eatin' fish as you'd ever want to see. As a rule I care for fish only to catch them, but that was one time I caught my fish and ate 'em too. Pompano, bluefish, and Spanish mackerel!

CHAPTER 12

Spinning on the Gulf Stream

I GET a good laugh every time I look back on my first experience at Gulf Stream spinning. Fishing with Captain Jack Reilly off Carysfort Light on Upper Key Largo, I was diligently casting and retrieving a white bucktail ahead of the *Swabbie* as Jack idled it along a weed line. Engrossed with watching the action of my lure, I blinked in disbelief when a huge, torpedo-like fish eased up and engulfed it. Setting the hook by reflex action, I found myself connected to one hundred pounds of Allison tuna by a wisp of six-pound-test nylon monofilament! The tuna, acting cool and collected about the whole thing, simply sounded slowly, methodically, and effortlessly. With all the confidence of a toothpick at a termite convention, I leaned back on the rod and poured the pressure on him.

Jack threw back his head and filled the air with riotous Irish laughter. "How much line ya' got?" he managed to ask.

"About two hundred yards," I allowed.

Tears of laughter streaming down his face, Jack roared, "That's not enough; it's seven hundred feet deep here!"

Sure enough, the tuna went straight down until all my line was gone, and that was that. But I'll always wonder what would have happened if I'd used a big reel and four hundred yards of line.

When you go to slinging spinning bucktails around in the Gulf Stream, there's no telling what may happen. You may run into horse-eye jacks no bigger than bluegills, or you may get a chance to cast your lure at a blue marlin as long as your boat. You may fish for hours and never get a strike, then suddenly find yourself surrounded by acres of ravenous dolphin or bonito. You never know what's liable to charge up out of the mysterious blue depths to grab your lure, but you can be sure that whatever latches on, you'll be in for an interesting battle.

Gulf Stream fish in general are of weak minds and strong backs, easy to hook but hard to handle. Most of them are Grade A suckers for spinning-size bucktails, but when the hook sinks home, they are wildcats dipped in turpentine.

The fish of the Gulf Stream are constantly on the move, running down flying fish, cruising in search of sardines, fleeing from bigger Gulf Stream fish, or simply fighting to hold their own against the waves and current. The mere routine of living in the Stream is a tough program of intensive physical training, and the fish that make the grade are a rugged lot indeed.

Not long ago, Johnny Herbert and I spotted a school of fish in the Gulf Stream off Elbow Reef on Key Largo. They had balled up a few thousand sardines into a tight wad, and were methodically chopping the wad into bite-size pieces.

Dozens of gulls screamed raucously overhead, diving for the sardines that tried to escape by jumping. The bulge-type rises of the feeding fish identified them as members of the bonito or tuna family.

Cautiously I eased the skiff close to the balled bait and shut off the motor. This was Johnny's first crack at the Gulf Stream, and he lost no time in getting his bucktail into the boiling mass of sardines. As I made my own cast I heard Johnny's reel break into a scream. I let my bucktail sink well below the ball of bait, but suddenly decided I'd better get it back into the boat so as not to endanger Johnny's chances through a possible line tangle. As I started to bring it in, however, a battering strike nearly took the rod out of my hands, and my reel joined Johnny's in a high-pitched discord of screaming.

Luckily, our fish ran in opposite directions, and our lines did not cross. As a matter of fact, by the time those two fish stopped running they were a good three hundred yards apart. Then they sounded, and for the next several minutes, Johnny and I had a strenuous time of it as we pumped them to the boat.

Johnny was first to work his fish close to the surface, and as he reached for the net he exclaimed, "Holy smoke! The damn' thing's only a minnow!"

The "minnow" took off again, however, and Johnny's tired wrists took another going over before he managed to bring the fish back to be netted. "And I thought jacks were tough," Johnny muttered.

Our fish turned out to be little tunas weighing about four and one-half pounds. By the time I landed mine, the rest of the school and their ball of sardines had disappeared. The gulls were gone, and not a swirl disturbed the placid surface of the water. But it was all right with us; we'd cruise about and find more fish, grateful for the rest to our weary wrists. That's the way it goes on the Gulf Stream.

Size considered, the little tunas and their bonito cousins are among the roughest and toughest of all Gulf Stream fish, and that's saying something. Shaped like aerial bombs, these solid chunks of muscle explode with almost as much violence when they feel the hook. Their runs are unbelievably powerful and sustained, and fast enough to make inshore speedsters like bonefish seem lethargic by comparison.

One day I was out on the Gulf Stream alone, having a go at a school of small rainbow runners. They weighed only about a pound apiece, and I had rigged up a light spinning outfit with a tiny size 4 bucktail tied directly to the five-pound test line. This rig made for a lot of sport with the rainbow runners, but I was unprepared when a four- or five-pound little tuna zoomed up and grabbed the lure. As he felt the hook he began to run, and as far as I know he's still running, with two hundred yards of five-pound monofilament flagging out behind. Of course, I might have saved the fish (and line) by cranking up the outboard to follow him, but I just wanted to see how much line he would take. Now I know.

The little tuna is not a small bluefin tuna, but a distinct species also known as "false albacore," or by the all-inclusive term "bonito." Reaching a top weight of about twenty-five pounds, the little tuna would be too tough for any tackle if he grew to the size reached by the bluefin.

Four members of the bonito and little tuna tribe are commonly encountered in the Gulf Stream off Florida: the little tuna, the oceanic bonito, the blackfin tuna or long-finned albacore, and the Atlantic bonito. These fish are similar in appearance, feeding habits, and fighting ability when hooked. Deep, sounding fighters, they all make tough adversaries on any tackle, yet may be handled with spinning gear if your line is long enough and your wrists strong enough. In Florida, particularly off the Keys, any of them may be caught spinning at any time of year along the edge of the Gulf Stream.

They'll hit just about anything in the way of a lure, but are especially fond of bucktail jigs in spinning sizes. Lure color doesn't mean a thing to them, but they are particular about retrieve speed. Charter boat operators in Florida slow down their trolling speed when they *don't* want to hook bonitos! A fast retrieve gets 'em. When there is no surface activity to reveal the location of little tunas or bonitos, they are best found by trolling at a fairly good clip along the edge of the Gulf Stream. Once a school is located you'll have no trouble picking them off by casting from a free-drifting boat.

The little tuna tribe is a bit brutal for my taste in fish for spinning tackle. Give me the gaudy and spectacular species, like dolphin. Beautiful and naive dolphin. My first experience with them is unforgettable.

It was a glassy calm day on the Gulf Stream, with bright sunshine and a nearly cloudless sky. The water was even bluer than usual . . . almost too blue to believe. Theoretically, it was a poor day for Gulf Stream fishing, but the weather was so good I just couldn't resist the temptation to make a long run out of sight of land in my new fourteen-foot Fiberglas boat. The Stream seemed dead as I crossed Elbow Reef, six miles off Key Largo, but I continued on and on, looking for some gulfweed or driftwood, which might shelter a few fish. Finally, about ten miles offshore, I found a mere thread of a weed line. Not much weed, but there were baby flying fish and other minnows in the shade of each tiny clump of it.

Reasoning that if there were any fish in the area at all, they'd be loitering near this food supply, I decided to troll along the weed line and hope for the best. Snapping a small white bucktail on my light wire leader, I payed out about thirty yards of line and went to trolling. As I eased along at about two or three knots, I constantly scanned the water surface for some sign of fish life, but not a swirl or bulge could I see. By chance I happened to glance down into the water beside the boat, and there swam a school of the most beautiful fish I'd ever seen, gliding along happily in the shade it offered. Dolphin!

Madly I began to reel in my bucktail to give them a look at it, but a smashing strike stopped me cold.

The fish fought hard and doggedly, making fast, short runs, and swirling at the surface from time to time, but made no jumps. This wasn't the way dolphin were supposed to act. Before long I had the answer. My dolphin was a barracuda. A doggone barracuda that had no business four miles off the outer reef picking up lures intended for more exotic game. But there he was, and there was not much I could do but fight him. 'Cudas can be tough customers on spinning gear, and this one turned out to be a brute.

He doggedly resisted my efforts to bring him to the net for ten or fifteen minutes, while I cussed him fervently and punished him to the limit of my tackle. At last he gave up, and when I got him in the net I realized why he gave me so much trouble. That 'cuda weighed nearly fifteen pounds. He had chewed up my lure and leader so badly that I had to replace them before taking a crack at the school of dolphin, but finally I was ready. I was ready, but the dolphin had wearied of waiting. They had disappeared.

Again I cranked up the outboard and idled along the weed line, not bothering to troll, and watched closely behind the boat for dolphin. Suddenly, I imagined I saw a flash of gold and blue; then I did see one. Then, magically, there were dolphin everywhere, under the boat and around it. I lobbed a short cast and watched breathlessly as dozens of dolphin converged on the lure, following its course through the air. The splashes of the bucktail and a striking dolphin merged into one, and then the fun began.

First the fish merely shook his head a few times as if trying to figure out what was sticking him. Then he soared three feet out of the water and shook all over, like a dog coming in from a swim. When this didn't free him, he decided to take drastic action. Away he zoomed on a run that literally sizzled, greyhounding as he went, and taking one hundred yards of line fast enough to heat the drag nut on my reel. Now he sounded a little, and I could feel him swapping ends and trying to roll in the line. He sounded deeper, bulldogging like a jack. Suddenly the line went slack, and my dolphin was out of the water again, and again, and again in a staccato series of spectacular leaps. He began to tire rapidly now, and soon I was able to pump him to the boat. A last-ditch jump carried him right into my net, a young bull about thirty inches long and weighing about five pounds.

For the next hour I fought dolphin, hooking one on every cast I made, and landing four females of about seven pounds each. I lost several, but it made no difference, because I couldn't get the bucktail back to the boat without hooking another. None of the females ran as fast as the bull I caught first, but all of them fought more doggedly. One of them jumped only once, and with the energy thus conserved battled me for fifteen minutes. This was the last fish I caught, for the school became bored during the drawn-out fight and moved on. I didn't care, however, as approaching squalls said it was time to head for shore.

Although dolphin are capable of giving fairly heavy trolling tackle a good workout, they are nevertheless excellent light-tackle fish, and made to order for spinning. While very powerful swimmers, they do not fight with sheer brute force like the jacks and bonitos, but rely instead on their flashing speed and maneuverability. They do not sound and sulk for long periods, and they don't ordinarily run great distances in one direction. They feint, and spar, and shake, and jump, then run a little and jump again. Few fish can approach them in jumping ability, change of pace, or straightaway speed.

Dolphin are the most beautiful fish in the sea, graceful in form and kaleidoscopically colored in unbelievable combinations of yellows, greens, blues and purples. Against the deep, clear blue of the Gulf Stream they present a sight that simply cannot be described in print. For dolphin alone, spinning in the Gulf Stream is more than worthwhile. I just can't get enough of them.

Even that glamour boy of the Stream, the sailfish, will readily hit a spinning bucktail, but hooking him is a tough proposition. A sail uses his bill as a club to maim his prey before taking it into his mouth, and one or two whacks at an artificial lure is all he needs to peg it for a phoney. At this writing, I have not had the good fortune to land a sailfish on an artificial lure and spinning gear, but I have had several strikes. Leroy Layne of Cleveland, Ohio, turned the trick in the 1954

Metropolitan Miami Fishing Tournament, knocking off a fifty-five-pounder on a cast-and-retrieved artificial lure and regulation spinning tackle. Layne spent several years trying to perform this feat, and his persistence finally paid off. Anyone can catch a sailfish with a spinning rod and reel and natural bait trolled from an outrigger, but it takes a nifty hunk of angling to catch one on a cast-and-retrieved artificial lure.

You do not need heavyweight spinning tackle for the Gulf Stream, as there's plenty of room to play your fish and never a necessity for snubbing them down during the fight. Principal tackle requirements are ample line capacity and a smoothly operating reel drag. The spinning rods the Florida boys use for Gulf Stream work weigh only about two and one-half ounces without fittings, and these are the same rods they use in fresh water and for inshore salt-water fishing. Such light rods are pleasant to use and remarkably efficient for wearing down hard-fighting fish, particularly when designed with fast tip action and reinforced, powerful butts.

The reel is unquestionably the most critical part of a Gulf Stream spinning outfit. Few reels will stand up to the kind of treatment Stream water and fish can hand out. Lukewarm and of high salinity, the water can rapidly turn a good reel into a piece of junk through corrosive action. Even reels that have proven themselves in inshore salt water may corrode when used in the Gulf Stream. Be sure that your reel has a stainless steel or equivalent bail and roller, and that all aluminum parts are properly anodized before you even go near the Gulf Stream with it. Be sure, too, that it has a smooth, dependable drag, a tough spool, and a sturdy rachet or antireverse lock. The need for high quality and rugged construction in a spinning reel for Stream use cannot be overemphasized. And while you're at it, you'd best be sure the reel you select will hold four hundred yards of six- or eight-pound Tynex monofilament.

While I use both six- and eight-pound-test monofilament for Gulf Stream spinning, I find myself gradually discarding the eight. Six-pound-test line casts much better than eight, particularly with one-eighth- to one-fourth-ounce lures, and there seems to be little difference in fish-holding properties . . . provided the reel drag does its job properly. Under no circumstances would I recommend using line heavier than eight-pound test, for the resulting loss in casting efficiency would more than offset the gain in strength.

An assortment of bucktail and nylon jigs in sizes 1 to 3/0 (one-eighth to one-half ounce) will just about cover the lure requirements for the Gulf Stream, but I like to carry a few top water plugs along just for laughs when dolphin show up. It's a lot of fun to see a dolphin soar out of the water twenty feet from the plug, and come down right on it! Light, braided stainless steel leaders about eighteen inches long should be used with any lure in the Gulf Stream, as most of the fish encountered are well fixed for sharp teeth.

More and more charter-boat skippers in Florida are recognizing the merits of spinning tackle for offshore fishing, and many of them are now specializing in this field. Captains Jack Reilly, of Upper Key Largo, and Eddie Edenfield, of Caribee Yacht Basin, Islamorada, are outstanding among the pioneers at this sport, and both are light-tackle specialists. Chartering with a skipper like Reilly or Edenfield is the surest way to success at Gulf Stream spinning; but for the most fun, try an outboard-powered skiff.

The Florida Keys area is well suited to offshore skiff fishing because there is neither surf nor a single dangerous inlet to fight on the way out and in. Squalls may be seen a long distance off, and there's plenty of time to head safely for shore if you keep your eyes open for them. In several summers of offshore skiff fishing, I've never been caught in a squall . . . and summer is the squally season in the Keys. For skiff work in the Gulf Stream, try to pick a day when the wind doesn't exceed fifteen miles per hour, and start out first thing in the morning. Chances are you'll get all the fishing you want by noon, before the afternoon squalls arrive. If possible, carry a spare motor. Even a little three-horse job will get you in if the big one conks out.

Finding the Gulf Stream is easy. Just head east until you hit the bluest water you've ever seen. Along the stretch from Miami to Palm Beach, it will usually run within two miles of the beach. In the Keys area, it my be scraping the outer reefs, or it may be a mile or two off them. In any case, you'll know it when you see it. Off Florida, the Gulf Stream is fifty miles wide and averages two thousand feet deep, so you can't possibly miss it.

In all that water, however, the finny population is well diluted, and you'll usually have to scout around a little to find fish. To do this, look for weed lines, which are nothing more than little floating clumps of yellow-brown gulfweed strewn out by the current or wind into broken lines. Weed lines are usually marked by slicks, which can be spotted a long way off in good weather. Weed lines harbor fish. Also keep your eyes peeled for birds, and if you see as many as three or four flying together, head for them. They group up only when they've found fish. And don't forget to watch the water around your boat. Gulf Stream fish are attracted to any floating object, your boat included.

You can nearly always find enough fish in the Gulf Stream to justify running out to it, and spinning's the way to get them. Even a beginner at the game can (and usually does) catch more fish than conventional Gulf Stream trollers, and he has infinitely greater sport doing it. Sailfish and marlin may get the publicity, but most of the Gulf Stream fish are of spinning-tackle size. The common ones are the dolphin, king mackerel, bonito, little tuna, rainbow runner, and assorted members of the jack family.

Of course, there's an ever present risk of hanging into large and extremely mettlesome fish when spinning in the Gulf Stream, and some of them are not exactly made to order for spinning tackle. This, to me, is the most appealing feature of Gulf Stream spinning. Besides the Allison tuna mentioned earlier, I have lost interesting bouts with wahoo, oversized dolphin, and big king mackerel . . . not to mention an occasional whopper of unidentified parentage. Losing such fish out of a skiff on spinning tackle is much more fun than landing them with seventy-two-pound-test line strung on a vaulting pole and 9/o reel in a fighting chair. And the fish you remember the longest are the big ones that got away!

CHAPTER 13

Mixed Bag from the Bays and Bridges

MANY of Florida's salt-water fish never make the outdoor magazines, or the press releases, or the chamber of commerce folders . . . but they do make a lot of fishermen happy. The fisherman who likes to fish for relaxation doesn't care much for wading a bonefish flat, casting a shore line for snook, or battling big, boisterous tarpon. He'd rather fish from an anchored boat in sheltered water, or from a bridge or pier, where he can soak up some Florida sunshine and catch a mess of panfish. The snappers, grunts, sheepshead, whiting, and their colleagues are always ready to do business with the casual fisherman who likes his fishing simple and easy. And some of the salt-water panfish, notably the snappers, can even prove exciting to the angler who fancies himself an expert.

Snapppers are the most interesting, and among the most plentiful, of Florida's relatively unpublicized game fish. Exceptionally hard fighters for their size, snappers are every bit as tough as the muscular jacks. Unlike the jacks, however, snappers have brains as well as brawn. Of some 150 different species of fresh- and salt-water fish with which I've had experience, the snappers are the smartest by far.

Cagiest of all the quick-witted snapper family is the mangrove snapper, most common of the lot in Florida—and maybe that's why he's so plentiful. The mangrove snapper is often carelessly referred to as a "red snapper," but the true red snapper is a relatively stupid fish found only in very deep, offshore waters. If you catch a snapper from inside waters, chances are it's a mangrove. Other snappers found in Florida are the schoolmaster, the lane snapper, the dog snapper, the muttonfish, and the yellowtail; but only the mangrove snapper occurs over the entire Florida coastline.

The mangrove snapper appears over deep and shallow reefs in the surf, in bays and lagoons, in creeks and rivers; and he even ascends into fresh water regularly. He loves cover, and, as his name implies, he will nearly always be found around mangrove roots along deep shore lines. Bridges, channel-markers, and piers are also to his liking.

The average mangrove snapper caught on hook and line will run less than a pound in weight, but a one-pounder is actually a naive youngster. Snappers become warier and wiser with every ounce of weight they put on, and by the time they grow to a couple of pounds they're pretty hard to fool. A typical twenty-pounder—sure, they get that big—could probably tell you the scientific name of the bait you use and the composition of the steel in your hook, if he could only talk. Very few mangrove snappers of adult size are caught by the average fisherman, yet snappers are so numerous that the little half-pounders are a major nuisance to live-bait fishermen in most South Florida waters.

On my first visit to the Keys I found out just how smart big mangrove snappers can be. There was a school of them lying under the dock near the fish-cleaning bench at Ev Fowler's Caribee Yacht Basin, and they were hungry and tame enough to come right to the surface for fish scraps. I bought a couple of mullet, cut them up, and began feeding the snappers. Big three- and four-pounders took the pieces of mullet just as fast as I threw them in. Then I put a hook in one of the mullet pieces and threw that in too, along with a couple of the un-attached chunks. The snappers gobbled up the free mullet, but—so help me—they wouldn't even approach the piece with the hook in it. The remarkable part of the whole thing was that I used a fly rod and a long six-pound-test leader with a small hook that was completely hidden by the bait. Again and again I tossed mullet chum to the snappers along with the baited hook, but not one fish made so much as a move toward my bait. Yet they continued to take the free chow just about as fast as it hit the water. Finally I gave up, tore the bait off my hook, and threw it to the fish. Yes, they snapped it up!

Dock snappers are the smartest of the smart, for they have to learn to recognize the hundreds of different kinds of baited hooks that thousands of fishermen dangle before them every year. Away from the boat and fish-cleaning docks, some big snappers can be fooled . . . sometimes. My first Keys experience to the contrary notwithstanding, the use of chum is one of the best ways to fool them. Toss bits of mullet or shrimp chum into the water a little at a time, until the snappers begin partaking of the free meal. (Florida's salt waters are usually clear enough for you to see the fish as they rise to the chum. In dark or murky waters, you'll just have to hope the chum is working.) As more and more fish join the chow line, increase the volume of chum until they seem to be competing recklessly for it. Without interrupting the chumming operation, toss in one piece with a hook attached. For best results, use monofilament nylon line with a small hook and without a leader or sinker. I have caught snappers up to three pounds by this method in locations where conventional fishing hardly ever takes them weighing over a pound. The effectiveness of chumming lies in its causing one fish to forget his natural caution in his haste to beat another to the free meal.

Chumming is a lot of bother, however, and there are other ways, too, to catch good-sized snappers. One method is to use a large hook (about a 4/0) and a big bait of cut mullet. Cast it out and let it go down. When the inevitable nibbles of small snappers start, ignore them; don't strike. If the nibbles stop, reel in, bait up again, and repeat the performance. Sooner or later a big snapper is going to grab that big bait away from the little ones, and when he grabs it, it won't feel like a nibble! The success of this method depends on NOT catching little snappers or even trying to hook them. The big fish stand back and let the little ones take the risks, and when they watch the youngsters gnaw on a big, juicy bait and get away with it, they figure it's safe. I first saw this method used by a bridge fisherman in the Keys, who took several mangrove snappers between two and four pounds one night, while I could get nothing but half-pounders on my little hook and small baits.

Another excellent and simple method that will take nice-sized snappers regularly is fishing with live shrimp on monofilament line without sinker or leader. It's best to use a small hook, no larger than a size 1 O'Shaughnessy (I prefer the smaller size 4), and hook the shrimp through the head just in front of the dark, opaque spot. Hooked in this manner, the shrimp can swim freely, and it looks much more natural than when threaded on the hook. Spinning tackle is ideal for fishing this simple rig, but light casting gear works pretty well, too. The important factor, of course, is the natural and detached appearance of the free-swimming shrimp on the small hook and monofilament line. The big disadvantage of this method is its overwhelming success on small snappers, which grab the shrimp before the big ones get a chance at it. Still, small snappers are nice panfish, so perhaps this disadvantage may be overlooked.

When it comes to artificial lures for snappers, small jigs and weighted bucktails are the best bet. Snappers like their jigs well chewed up and bedraggled rather than in new condition, and they seem to prefer yellow or blue to all other colors. The biggest mangrove snapper I've ever caught hit a blue number 1 Upperman bucktail that was so beaten up that Bill Upperman himself wouldn't have recognized it. The snapper, incidentally, went over four pounds.

Bucktail, feather, and nylon jigs are especially effective for snappers in swash channels, along mangrove shore lines, around bridge abutments, and in the sand-bottomed potholes of grass flats. Rocky bottoms or coral reefs, while good spots, are difficult to fish properly with jigs because snappers like their lures bounced off the bottom. This is true even in shallow water, and not merely the case in deep fishing for deep-lying fish. Snappers will nearly always go down for a lure more readily than they'll come up for it. At times, however, they will hit surface lures along the mangroves.

Mangrove snappers are fun to catch and fine to eat . . .

worthy fish from any angle. And if you want to give your angling skill the acid test, see what you can do with snappers weighing more than two pounds. The little ones are no problem; anyone can take them readily from any South Florida bridge.

Florida probably has more bridges spanning salt water than any other state, and these bridges, along with the many piers and jetties that stud the coast line, have a great deal to offer the casual fisherman. If you don't care for boats, or fancy tackle, or esoteric angling methods, all you have to do is bait a hook with cut shrimp or mullet, live shrimp, or a fiddler crab, and drop it off the nearest bridge. In no time at all you'll feel the bite of a sheepshead, grunt, snapper, grouper, or some other hungry bottom fish. Highly popular in the Sunshine State, bridge- and pier-fishing are very good bets for the tourist who may lack the knowledge of the water necessary for success in fishing from a boat without a guide. And you never know about bridge- or pier-fishing. There's always a chance that you'll hang onto more than you bargained for. Big snook, tarpon, drum, cobia, and gigantic jewfish all like to hang around bridges. Jacks, ladyfish, mackerel, bluefish, channel bass, sea trout, or pompano may appear at any time to grab a bridge-fisherman's bait. Bridge-fishing in Florida can be (and usually is) quite an adventure.

Probably the best bait (and also the most expensive) for bridge-fishing is live shrimp, for this is a principal natural food of nearly all salt-water fish in subtropical waters. Prices for live shrimp range from twenty-five to fifty cents a dozen, with jumbos running as high as ten cents apiece. At these prices, bridge-fishing can become an expensive proposition where bait-stealing sheepshead, swellfish, and small snappers abound.

For this reason, most Florida bridge-fishermen use cut mullet or dead shrimp. Sand fleas and fiddler crabs are also widely used, particularly when the quarry is sheepshead.

Mullet may be purchased at any Florida bait shop or fish market for about thirty or thirty-five cents per pound. To prepare cut baits, first scale the mullet, then fillet it as you would for table use. The fillets may then be cut into bait-size pieces, the size depending on the size of your hook and the fish you're after. Be sure that the skin remains on each bait you cut, for it is the skin that holds the bait on the hook. The head of the mullet is also good bait, especially for grouper and big snapper, and the backbone and innards make good chum. Cut mullet is an excellent all-round bait for most of the panfish and many of the game fish that hang around piers and bridges. In Florida, nearly all fish like mullet.

Mullet is usually fished right on bottom, with an egg sinker on the line above the leader. The size of the sinker to use depends on the speed of the tide and the water depth, since it's best to use the minimum weight that will hold the bait down. An egg sinker permits the line to slide through the hole that runs lengthwise through this type of weight, offering minimum resistance to a light-biting or suspicious fish. This is much like the fish-finder rig mentioned in Chapter 9, but the egg sinker is superior to the fish-finder's pyramid for bridge-fishing because it doesn't hang up on rocky bottom so readily.

For hand-line fishing from bridges or piers, the best rig is the one with the hooks above the sinker. This arrangement gives the hand-line fisherman a better chance to feel his bites and hook his fish. Bank sinkers from two to four ounces in weight are best for this rig. It pays to use two 1/o hooks, each on a wire or nylon snell. The lower hook should swing just above the sinker, and the upper hook about a foot or so above the lower one. Many fishermen bait one hook with cut mullet and the other with cut shrimp, thereby giving the fish a degree of choice for their final meal. Of course, any natural bait may be used with a hand line, but delicate and easily stolen baits like live shrimp or fiddler crabs are best fished with rod and reel.

Fiddler crabs are easily caught along the shores of creeks and bays at low tide. Remove the large claw, and hook the crab through the back part of the shell. This is the best bait you can get for the bridge-loving sheepshead, but must be fished with a special technique to thwart the bait-stealing skill of these fish. Simply baiting up and letting the sinker carry the baited hook down to the bottom is a good way to fatten sheepshead, but not to catch them. It's best to use fiddlers on a fairly light rod, reel, and line . . . like a fresh-water bait-casting outfit. Slip an egg sinker on the line, then tie on a swivel to keep the sinker from sliding off. Fasten a foot or so of nylon or steel leader on the swivel, and use a well-honed size 1 O'Shaughnessy hook. After baiting with a fiddler crab, allow the sinker to carry the bait straight down to bottom near a bridge piling, then raise it so that the hook just clears the bottom, the weight of the sinker keeping the line taut. This will enable you to feel the very sly tugs of a biting sheepshead. When the slightest tug occurs, lower the rod tip with it, and then strike hard. If you do not hold the hook and sinker off bottom, the sheepshead will steal your fiddler crabs as fast as you can bait up . . . and you'll never feel them bite! Fiddler crabs, incidentally, are also good bait for the triggerfish, drum, and small jewfish that loaf around the pilings of many Florida bridges.

Live shrimp, of course, may be fished on the regular bottom rig as used for cut mullet, but this isn't the way to get the most out of such an attractive bait. Much better is the unweighted-line method of drifting the shrimp with the current on a slack line. Many Florida bridge-fishermen use a bobber when baiting with live shrimp, letting it float out with the tide a few feet beneath the surface. This keeps the shrimp out of reach of bothersome little grunts, snappers, sea catfish and other bottom fish, and gives such near-surface feeders as sea trout, mackerel, and bluefish a chance to have a go at it.

The big, expensive jumbo shrimps make excellent bait for the whopper snook that lie under many South Florida bridges, but the little fish can really raise cain with your jumbo shrimp supply if you don't guard against them. The best way to fish big live shrimp for bridge snook is to use a stout cane pole about ten feet long with an equal length of heavy wire line and about a 5/0 hook. Hook the shrimp through the head in front of the opaque spot, and lower it into the water as close as possible to the bridge on the uptide side, so that it drifts under the bridge. Keep it well off the bottom away from the panfish, and keep it moving, working it slowly back and forth and up and down. KEEP A FIRM GRIP ON THE POLE. When a snook strikes, lay the pole to him with all you've got, and get him out from under the bridge. With so-called sporting tackle you haven't a chance of getting a big snook past the barnacle-encrusted pilings, but the cane pole and wire line even things up a bit. And before you start feeling sorry for the snook caught on such tackle, just try handling a twenty-pounder from a bridge with a ten-foot cane pole!

Bridges, piers, sea walls and jetties, of course, make good vantage points for the artificial-lure fisherman, particularly for mackerel, bluefish, pompano, jacks and ladyfish. Many bridge-fishermen keep a casting or spinning outfit rigged and ready so that they can lay down their bait rigs and go to casting when a school of surface-feeding fish comes by. Others fish only artificials from the bridges and jetties, piling into their cars to move from one bridge to another until they find fish. Bridge hopping is practical in many coastal areas of Florida, for the bridges are many and not too far between. As a matter of fact, Florida bridge-hopping specialists get to know the game so well that they are able to take advantage of the tide time lag between bridges, and rush from one spot to another to hit the tide just right at each spot.

Coming into great popularity with Florida bridge-fishermen for everything from hand lines to light casting rigs are monofilament nylon lines in tests from ten to sixty pounds. Monofilament has much lower visibility in the water, wears well, doesn't chafe so readily on pilings, and requires considerably less sinker weight to hold it down in a strong tide than a conventional line. Other factors being equal, monofilament line will increase your bridge catch by 20 per cent over old-fashioned twisted or braided line.

Some of Florida's best bridge- and pier-fishing is to be had at night, when the crowds thin out and the fish become less cautious. Snappers, grunts, snook, jacks, ladyfish, sea trout, and many other species feed actively after dark; more actively, in many cases, than during daylight hours. Night bridge-fishing is fascinating, productive, and extremely pleasant on warm winter nights when the mosquitoes and sand flies aren't too active. For night fishing, use the same gear and baits you'd use in the daytime, but be sure to carry a lantern and a good insect repellent. Never shine your light on the water; just use it for baiting up and unhooking your fish, and as a signal to warn passing cars of your presence on the bridge.

An important accessory carried by many serious-minded Florida bridge-fishermen is a flying gaff rig, consisting of a huge treble hook tied to a length of nylon clothesline, for landing heavy fish. These hooks are available in most Florida tackle stores, and they sure are handy when the time comes to get that big one up on the bridge.

The best way to learn about Florida bridge- and pier-fishing is to try it, and to talk to other bridge- and pier-fishermen. Many fishermen make a specialty of this kind of fishing, and some are highly skilled and resourceful experts in the same sense that some dry-fly men and some bait-casters are experts. The confirmed bridge-fisherman with years of experience behind him can catch fish when conditions are such that the tyro is convinced there are no fish to be caught. And the nice thing about expert bridge-fishermen is that they are sociable guys and gals, who tend to be much more generous about sharing their knowledge than the experts in other fields of angling endeavor.

Salt-water panfishing and bridge-fishing are synonomous in Florida, although not all panfishing is done from bridges, nor is all bridge-fishing panfishing. But nearly every bridge spanning salt water in Florida does offer good panfishing, while it would be stretching the truth to claim that all bridges yield substantial numbers of the larger game fish. For bridge-fishing at its best, whether it's panfish or lunkers you're after, try the Overseas Highway (now toll free) on the Florida Keys.

CHAPTER 14

Largemouth Bass, Florida Division

BEFORE I came to Florida to live I had often heard it said that, while Florida bass were big, they were poor fighters: pot-bellied and slow, like old, waterlogged shoes snagged from a creek bottom. Well, the first thing I did after landing in Clewiston and checking into a motel was try a little bass fishing in Lake Okeechobee, and it didn't take me long to realize that Florida largemouths were as game as any largemouths I'd met in the seven or eight other states in which I'd caught them. Now that I've caught literally thousands of Florida bass, I believe they're actually harder fighters, on the average, than their Northern cousins.

Just how this erroneous notion about the Florida largemouth's fighting ability ever got started I don't know, but I imagine it stems from a sour-grapes attitude on the part of Northern bass fishermen. It is, after all, consoling to think that "Florida bass don't fight, anyway" when your own bass pond is iced in for the winter!

Florida bass fishing varies from good to bad, like bass fishing everywhere, but when it's good, it may well be fantastic. Too good to be true, and even too good to be interesting. I caught so many bass during my first year as a Florida resident that I grew sick and tired of them, but then the fishing around Clewiston dropped off for a couple of years as a result of huge fish kills by severe hurricanes, and my interest picked up again. Bass fishing right now is good, but not boringly so, as it was back in 1947—when I once landed bass weighing two pounds or better on thirty-eight consecutive casts! And frankly, I hope it never gets that "good" again.

There are two principal kinds of largemouth bass in Florida: the common largemouth, *Micropterus salmoides*, and a subspecies, *Micropterus salmoides floridanus*, the Florida largemouth. These fish have the same habits and habitats, and for practical purposes may be considered as one. Certain differences in appearance are evident, however; and if you'd like to be able to tell them apart, you can write the Game and Fresh Water Fish Commission at Tallahassee for reprint of "Identifying the Florida Basses," by John F. Dequine.

Florida has so much bass water that it's a major problem to decide where to go for a bass fishing vacation. If you fished in a different lake, stream, or canal every day, it would take you eighty-five years to wet a line in every body of bass water! Each section of Florida claims that it has the best bass fishing in the world, and chances are that each has . . . for the fishermen who know the local waters. Such famous bass spots as Leesburg, Orlando, Eustis, Lakeland, Welaka, and the towns of the Lake Okeechobee area play host to repeat visitors year after year, each satisfied that the fishing spot of his choosing provides the best possible bass fishing. The fact of the matter is that you can't go wrong in Florida when it's bass you're looking for. Just pick a place you like and stick with it. The fishing will seem to get better and better each year, as you become more familiar with the waters and the habits of the particular bass that swim in them.

Florida's bass waters are almost as varied in type as they are numerous, ranging from swift streams to deep, crystal lakes; dark cypress ponds; lazy rivers; huge, shallow grass beds; drainage canals; and even potholes. The largemouth bass, being one of the most adaptable of all fresh-water fish, naturally forms habits befitting the environment in which he finds himself. To do business with him in Florida, then, you'll have to give some thought to the type of water you're fishing, and fish it accordingly. All of the bass fishing methods in general use throughout the country will work in Florida, and only experience will teach you how to apply the method you prefer to Florida conditions.

Bait-casting is still the most popular bass-fishing method in Florida, but fly-fishing is closing in fast. Native Florida bass fishermen are, by and large, the doggonedest bunch of surface-lure addicts to be found anywhere, and floating fly-rod bugs, in particular, have really caught their fancy during the last few years. Bug fishing is productive at some time or other in every type of water Florida has to offer.

While bass-bugging is commonly thought to be a recent development in Florida bass fishing, it is a matter of record that the Seminole Indians used crude deer-hair bugs for bass in Florida 'way back around the year 1700. You can bet that the Indians had no torpedo-head fly lines, glass rods, or automatic reels for their bug-fishing, but their deer-hair lures caught bass nevertheless. Florida bass still like bugs today . . . perhaps even better than they did in 1700 A.D.

Today bass bugs have reached a lofty state of development, and are produced in a great number of styles to cover a variety of fly-fishing needs. The bass bug may be an imitation mouse, frog, moth, minnow, or fly; or it may be an outlandish popper that makes no pretense at imitating anything. It may be made of deer hair, rubber, cork, balsa wood, or plastic. Defined loosely, a bass bug is any surface lure designed to be used with a fly rod.

The nicest thing about bass bugs is their appeal to Florida bass. There is something about a high-floating, natural-looking bug that bass find hard to resist, even when they're not particularly hungry. And the bass—bless him—is at his striking and fighting best when taken on a fly rod and top-water lure.

Deer-hair bugs have tremendous bass appeal, probably because of their natural soft feel and appearance. When a fish takes a hair lure, he actually munches it for several seconds before ejecting it as a phoney. Naturally, this feature makes for good hooking characteristics—if the bug is tied to give ample hook clearance. I'm partial to the mouse style of hair lure, particularly for shore-line fishing in very calm and glassy water. The hair mouse should be fished as slowly as possible, without much jerking. The various hair moths and frogs, too, are excellent, but all hair lures have one rather serious shortcoming; they soak up water and lose their buoyancy.

For maximum floatability of hair bugs, dip them in a solution of paraffin in white gasoline or benzene, and put them aside until thoroughly dry. The paraffin coats and seals each hair, keeping the water out for as long as a couple of hours of fishing. False casting to remove clinging water drops between each cast will help keep these lures floating even longer.

There are several types of hard-bodied bugs, all of which will take their shares of bass. Easily the most popular of these in Florida is the popper. Poppers come in many sizes and shapes, but they all have one feature in common: the concave face, which makes a popping sound when the bug is twitched. At times, poppers can be the most effective of bass lures, but there are occasions when the noisy ones seem to frighten rather than attract the fish. A popper, however, doesn't have to be popped, and the retrieve may be kept reasonably quiet if the bass want it that way. Whether it is popped loudly, moderately, or not at all, a popping bug should be fished very slowly for maximum effect on bass. A pause of at least several seconds should be allowed between pops to give an interested fish a chance to hit the lure. If he happens to be scrutinizing it closely, a loud pop is likely to scare him away. While bass will often hit a rapidly worked popper, they will take a slowly worked one much more often. It is practically impossible to fish a popper too slowly for bass.

Another popular type of hard-bodied bug is the feather minnow. If I had to limit myself to just one fly-rod surface lure for Florida bass fishing, my one lure would be a blue and white feather minnow tied on a size 2 or 4 hook. Feather minnows are supposed to imitate minnows, as the name implies. I doubt that many bass are actually fooled by such a crude imitation, but fooled or not, they certainly go for these lures.

A wide variety of actions can be imparted to the feather minnow: darting, struggling, skittering along the surface, or merely crawling along. Generally, the darting action—which is accomplished by short, intermittent jerks—is the best bass-producer; but you never can tell about the moods of bass, and it pays to experiment. As with the popper, a slow retrieve usually works best with the feather minnow, but this is not always the case. A fast retrieve is sometimes well received. In any event, a feather minnow may be worked very rapidly without danger of scaring the fish, while this is not always the case with poppers.

The winged or moth-type bass bug is less popular in Florida than either the popping bug or the feather minnow, but it is a killing lure nevertheless. It should be tied with the wings well balanced and not too large, or it may give considerable trouble in casting.

There is little question that a quivering or fluttering action is the best for winged bugs. They should be fished very slowly, and with very little retrieve. A moth or bug doesn't cover much distance in the water after falling in; it struggles and flutters, but doesn't seem to get anywhere. This is the action you should strive for when fishing a winged bass bug. Winged bugs are especially good for shore-line fishing late in the evening, when insects are flying and the water is smooth.

This is not a complete list of bass-bug types useful in Florida fishing . . . not by a long shot. Nevertheless, these principal styles of bug will cover nearly any situation encountered. The frog, crawfish, dragonfly, and other imitations are all good, but they are not absolutely necessary for success in Florida waters. Generally speaking, the best seasons for bug-fishing in Florida are spring, summer, and fall.

If you're willing to fish underwater flies from time to time, you'll find that one of the best of all fly-rod bass lures for Florida, or anywhere else for that matter, is a fly-and-spinner combination. Either a bucktail or hackle fly will do, with an over-all length of about two inches, tied on a size 1 or 1/0 ringed hook. The spinner should not be too large—a size 1 Idaho or Indiana is about right—for a large spinner is

Four-pound Florida largemouth from Fisheating Creek, west of Lake Okeechobee. The Florida largemouth is a subspecies of largemouth bass, distinctly different from northern bass.

This is a Lake Okeechobee hayfield, a vast area of needle grass, saw grass, and lily pads growing in about three feet of water. A skilled fisherman can fish his weedless lures through the thickest growth, and get more bass than the fellow who fishes only the open spots.

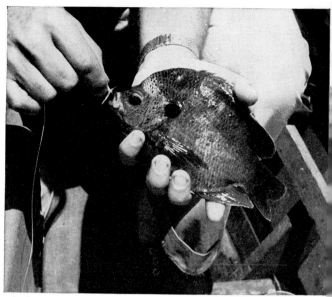

Florida bluegills run fat and sassy . . . loads of fun on a light fly rod. This one took a tiny popping bug.

The most insignificant looking canals in Florida produce good panfishing. The author's daughter plays a big warmouth hooked on a spinning bucktail.

Weedless hooks like these may be used to fish frog-shaped pork chunks through the dense weed growths that are so heavily populated by Florida bass.

'Owl-Eye" bucktails as described in Chapter 15 are excellent spinning lures for both fresh- and salt-water panfish. These lures are unbeatable for warmouth.

Florida fishing is relatively unspoiled by civilization, even in the metropolitan areas. Manny Eisfeld lands a lookdown from Biscayne Bay, within view of downtown Miami.

The author's son casting in a typically beautiful Florida river, the Caloosahatchee. This section is fresh water, but along with the fresh-water fish there are tarpon and snook

hard to cast and manipulate with a fly rod. Fished with a darting, jerk-and-pause action, this lure will take bass when everything else fails. Fly-and-spinner rigs are especially good around the edges of lily pads, cypress knees and similar cover commonly found in Florida waters. (Incidentally, you do not need a fly rod to take bass with a fly and spinner, for this is a wonderful cane-pole dibbling lure, which will really bring the bass out from under the lily pads when worked back and forth persistently along the edges.) Combinations of yellow, white, and red are good colors for spinner flies in most Florida waters.

Some of Florida's best bass fishing is to be had in very shallow water, like the extensive flats in Lake Okeechobee and the gently sloping shore lines of many of the lakes in the central part of the state. Nowhere else have I found bass fishing quite like the shallow-water fishing to be found in Florida, so perhaps we'd better look into a few of the effective techniques involved.

Generally speaking, when a bass enters water no more than two feet in depth he has the same thing in mind that you have when you stroll into a resturant. He's hungry, and he knows he'll find a meal in the shallows. Perhaps he'll be in a finicky mood and want to look over the various entrees of minnows, crayfish, frogs, or shrimp before deciding on a first course; or maybe he'll take 'em as they come, figuring that a meal in the gullet is worth two in the waterweeds. In either mood, the bass in the shallows is a pushover for the angler who knows how to fish for him.

In fishing for shallow-water bass, it must be constantly borne in mind that the fish are instinctively on guard, keeping watchful eyes peeled for ospreys, 'gators, water snakes, otters, and other natural enemies to which their exposed position makes them vulnerable. Sloppy casting, loud-splashing plugs, or unnecessary thumpings or scrapings in the boat will send Mr. Bass scurrying for the safety of the depths. He can't afford to take any chances; nature's law of self-preservation forbids it. (Perhaps you have run into shallow-water bass that seemed utterly without caution. So have I, but these foolhardy fish are exceptions, whose human counterparts are steeplejacks, circus performers, and guys who write fishing books.)

Necessary for success with bass in thin water, then, are a careful approach and a light casting touch. Move slowly; fish are less likely to detect slow, deliberate motions than quick ones. Do not try to reach the fish with record-breaking casts. It is much better to maneuver close enough for a smooth and easy eighty-foot heave if using a casting or spinning rod, and to within no more than forty to fifty feet with a fly rod. The best way to approach a feeding bass in shoal water is by wading, but a poled—not rowed or paddled—boat can be placed close enough to the fish to put the most modestly capable caster in business.

Choice of an outfit for fishing the shallows depends mainly on the nature of the water. For areas that are fairly clear of weeds, the fly rod is probably the most formidable weapon, with the spinning outfit a close second. Where a heavy weed growth exists, however, the bait-casting outfit is most practical. These recommendations are based on a couple of important reasons. In the first place, you'll find that bass in open shallows tend to be so jumpy that the splash of a casting-size lure may flush them . . . at least some of them. The delicate little splat of a fly or tiny spinning lure, on the other hand, bothers them not a bit. Not that casting lures won't take bass in the open shallows, for they certainly will . . . but flies and spinning lures will take more.

In weedy waters, bass evidently feel that they're hidden from their enemies, and seem to be far less skittish. Large plugs or spoons do not panic them here unless landing right on top of them. The advantage of casting tackle for weed fishing lies in the greater strength of the tackle, enabling you to haul the bass clear of the weeds before the line or leader is fouled. This doesn't mean that fly and spinning tackle won't handle bass in grassy shallows, but only that casting gear will land a larger percentage of strikes in such water.

I am partial to small lures for shallow-water bass fishing —or any kind of shallow-water fishing, for that matter. The usual food a bass is apt to find in water less than two feet deep runs small: insects, small minnows, small frogs, small crayfish. He's looking for something small when he enters the shoals, so why not serve it up to him? Then too, of course, there is the matter of greater delicacy and less noise in casting small lures. Though running a severe spinning fever these days, I still prefer the fly rod for thin-water bass. If bass are in the shallows at all, it is a rare thing for them to refuse a properly worked bass bug.

One word of caution regarding the use of bugs, or any other surface lure, in very shallow water. DO NOT TRY TO SET THE HOOK TOO QUICKLY AT THE STRIKE. There will usually be a well-defined wake when a fish comes for the lure. Give him time to take it before striking. This may seem like a foolish warning, but you'd be surprised how your reflexes can cross you up when the heavy wake of a big Florida bass closes in on your lure!

Top lures for spinning in the shallows are the cute little miniature replicas of standard surface casting lures. They may be dropped on the water with very little splash, and the combination of a long, light rod and thin line allows them to be worked beautifully. Another killer for the spinning outfit is a small pork chunk on a weedless hook. Florida bass really go for pork, and more about that later.

Despite the rising popularity of spinning and fly-fishing in Florida, there are probably more bass taken with casting tackle than by all other methods combined . . . and casting tackle will take its share of shallow-water bass. Here again, surface lures are probably most productive, but where the weeds are thick, any of the old reliable weedless spoons will often turn the trick when everything else fails.

Many of Florida's best bass waters are weedy beyond the conception of the average Northern fisherman, and it was in these waters that many of the country's best-known weedless lures were developed. While you may prefer shore-line or open-water fishing to dredging the weeds for bass, weed fishing is absolutely necessary a good share of the time if you want to put bass in the boat. Florida bass fishermen, especially in the Lake Okeechobee area, are the most highly skilled I've ever seen when it comes to working weedy waters. Their principal lures for the weeds and grass beds are variations on a pork-rind theme.

I'll never forget an old Cracker fisherman I met shortly after coming to Florida. He had a cane pole in one hand and a string of the most beautiful bass I'd ever seen in the other as he trudged up from the meadow banks of lower Fisheating Creek.

"That sure is a nice mess of bass," I remarked. "What did you get 'em on?"

"Meat skin and red yarn," he grinned.

"Meat skin" is simply a Cracker term for pork rind, but no matter what you call it, there's nothing else quite so effective for luring Florida bass out of a weed bed. Most Florida bass fishermen use their pork rind on weedless spoons, fished right through the thickest vegetation.

While a few bass can be taken by casting a spoon and pork rind into the open spots in a grass bed, this technique doesn't produce more than a small fraction of the strikes the Florida boys get by fishing the thick stuff. The trick involved here is to gauge the retrieve so that the lure slithers over the heavy growth and slips into the water whenever it comes to even the smallest open spot. The first time you fish a Lake Okeechobee "hayfield" you'll find that this is more difficult than it sounds, for the needle grass will actually hold the lure above the water throughout the retrieve until you get the hang of it. By holding the rod tip high to keep the line clear of the grass, working the tip gently to slide the spoon around and over the tough spots, and slowing the retrieve to permit the lure to sink into each open patch of water it crosses, you'll soon find yourself doing a good job of weed-fishing without getting hung up too often. And you'll find yourself catching far more bass than you'd ever get by sticking to the open areas.

Even better than a weedless spoon and pork rind for fishing thick weed beds is a frog-shaped pork chunk on a plain weedless hook, as mentioned in Chapter 8. The best type of hook is an inexpensive style, the weed guard of which actually encloses the barb. (See Illustration 15 top). Size 2/0 is about right for a standard quarter-ounce frog chunk. Spinning tackle is ideal for casting pork frogs, but it pays to use a six- or eight-foot length of ten- or twelve-pound-test monofilament on the end, to absorb the punishment of being dragged through the grass.

Frog chunks are just the right weight for spinning gear,

and may be cast into the thickest weeds with little danger of hanging up. Bass will often snap up a pork frog when the flash of a spoon causes them to shy away. Fish the chunk slowly through the grass, working the rod tip gently to give it as much wiggle as possible. When a bass hits, give him a second or two to get the lure in his mouth, then strike him hard. Pork chunks feel so natural that bass will actually mouth them for some time before spitting them out.

Shallow and weedy waters aren't the only places to look for bass in Florida. At times it pays to fish the deeper lakes right out in the middle, with lures that really go down. A few years ago I was fishing a small lake in the city limits of Lakeland with Paul Mains, outdoor columnist for the Jacksonville paper, *The Florida Times-Union.* The occasion was the spring meeting of the Florida Outdoor Writers Association. Paul and I were out before breakfast trying to win a trophy, which was to be given by the Lakeland Chamber of Commerce for the biggest bass caught from a city lake by one of the writers. After an hour or so of shore-line fishing, we were still looking for our first strike.

"Let's row out in the middle," Paul suggested, "and fish deep."

Without much hope, we made a drift over the deep water, casting at random with deep-running lures. Still no action. Just as a gag, I hauled out the most outlandish plug in my tackle box, a black-and-red-spotted orange thing shaped like a football with a large metal lip. Holding it up for Paul to see, I said, "Somebody up at Heddon must have had a hangover when he designed this, but Homer Circle sent it to me, and said it runs deep. They call it a Go-Deeper Crab."

Paul made an appropriate quip, laughed, and went on

casting his conservative plug. I snapped on the big plug and went to work with it. My first retrieve dredged some weeds from the bottom, so at least the plug was going down where I wanted it. The other plugs we'd tried didn't even get weeds. Several more casts scraped moss off the bottom, and then darned if I didn't hang a fish.

"Keep that one," ordered Paul. "He looks like a winner."

I boated the fish, and managed to take and release two more on the goofy plug before we had to quit for breakfast. When we returned to the Lakeland Terrace Hotel, Paul slipped into the kitchen to ice my bass, then announced to the gang that I had caught a bass estimated to weigh seven pounds, two ounces. As it turned out at the official weigh-in, Paul's guess was a wee bit optimistic, but my sixteen and one-half ounce bass did win the trophy. No one else caught a fish, probably because no one else dredged bottom with such a crazy-looking lure.

Prior to that experience in Lakeland, I had given little thought to fishing deep for bass in Florida, but since then I have taken many bass right off the bottom in fifteen to thirty feet of water. The deep lakes in the central part of the state will often yield splendid catches of bass to the fisherman who's willing to go deep for them when they leave the shore lines and weed beds, while the average fisherman goes strikeless and chalks the fish off as not hitting.

Deep, slow trolling over deep water is an excellent way to locate bass when they are not in evidence along the shore lines, and this method is popular in North Central Florida. Once you hook a fish by trolling, you can cast over the area with deep-running plugs with a good chance of further action. Incidentally, salt-water jigs and bucktails are hard to beat for bass in deep water, actually doing a better job than most conventional deep-running bass lures. Fish the jigs as described in Chapter 1, bouncing them off the bottom with a slow, whippy retrieve.

Typical of many pleasant experiences I've had with saltwater jigs and bass in Florida was the one a friend and I recently had in Lake Okeechobee. We planned to spend an afternoon on one of the grass beds several miles off shore, but a strong wind forced us to turn back. For want of something better to do, we decided to try the deep water of the rim canal, which runs along the entire south shore of Okeechobee and is sheltered by the hurricane levee on one side and a spoil bank on the other. An hour or so of shore-line fishing with conventional lures and methods didn't even give us a strike, but before giving up we voted to try the mouth of a deep cut leading from the canal through the spoil bank to the lake proper. Snapping on weighted bucktails, we went to jigging, saltwater style. Casting across the mouth of the cut, we'd jig our lures to within a rod's length of the boat, then simply jig them up and down, letting them hit bottom after each whip of the rod. It would take a minute or two of the up-and-down jigging to make the bass blow their tops . . . then socko!—one of us would get a strike. As soon as one bass was hooked, another would hit the other fellow's jig. We had a lot of fun jigging up those bass, and there was considerable satisfaction in bringing in a limit catch when the weather was so unfavorable that practically no one else got any fish at all.

Bass don't quit feeding entirely when they go to deep water, but they do get lazy and somewhat indifferent to food. Nevertheless, they are nearly always susceptible to teasing, and there's nothing like a jig to tease them when they're lying on bottom. A drowsy bass might watch a plug pass just over his head time after time without losing his temper, but he just can't stand seeing a jig dance around him for long.

All of the nationally advertised bass lures will take their shares of Florida bass, and your own favorites will probably do a good job for you unless they happen to be unsuitable for the water you want to fish. You couldn't expect to catch bass with a River Runt in a Lake Okeechobee hayfield, for example, simply because you couldn't possibly make a retrieve. Yet the River Runt will prove an excellent lure for the open waters of the clear lakes through the citrus belt. Carry a varied assortment of lures for your fly, spinning, or casting outfit, and don't be afraid to experiment if the bass don't seem too enthusiastic about your first offering. I have seen tourist fishermen new to Florida waters catch more bass than experienced Florida guides, simply because the guides were "sot in their ways," while the tourists experimented with different lures.

Most of the giant-sized bass for which Florida is famous are taken with live bait from the lakes in the central and northern part of the state. The favored live bait is a big shiner—the bigger the better—fished in the lily pads under a large float. Many bass weighing nearly twenty pounds are taken each year by native cane-polers in this manner, but these fish never make the headlines or the *Field & Stream* contests. The Florida Crackers who catch them aren't interested in contests; they're after meat on the table. Besides, *Field & Stream*'s contest rules state that the entry must be caught on rod, reel, and line . . . not a cane pole. Even with the biggest ones left out, however, mighty few bass from outside Florida could ever get as much as an honorable mention in *Field & Stream*'s contest for largemouth bass, Florida division.

When bass fishing in Florida you may hang into an occasional prehistoric-looking gar or mudfish. These rough fish have become a serious problem in certain Florida lakes and canals, competing with bass for food and in some cases actually using bass for food. Mudfish, or bowfins, and gars are poor game fish and even worse food fish. When you catch one, keep your fingers clear of his jaws while you remove the hook, then kill him with a blunt instrument before tossing him overboard. By destroying these rough fish you'll be doing the bass a favor.

CHAPTER 15

Fresh-Water Panfish

I watched Manny's cast settle lightly on the slick surface of the water, and a moment later heard the typical kissing sound of a rising bluegill. Manny's light fly rod slanted into a graceful curve as the fish bored in darting circles, doggedly attempting to pull away from the hook. A few moments later his face beamed with a happy grin as he held up a chunky bluegill.

"This is my idea of fishin', Phil," he said. "You can have your snook, and your tarpon, and your bass; I'll take brim!"

Manny thinks nothing of driving a two hundred-mile round trip from Miami to Clewiston for a whack at Lake Okeechobee panfish. Like thousands of other anglers in Florida, he finds a peaceful relaxation in panfishing that angling for the more boisterous game fish does not offer.

While Florida's reputation as the top fishing state in the

country is founded primarily on its salt-water fishing and secondarily on its bass fishing, Florida's fresh-water panfishing is even more remarkable. One out of every twelve acres of inland Florida is fresh water, and there are panfish galore in every body of it. It is impossible to stay on Florida's mainland and get farther than eighteen miles from a lake, stream, or canal that offers good panfishing!

Florida's principal panfish are all members of the sunfish family, a highly prolific tribe of spunky little scrappers. Most important are the bluegill; the stumpknocker, or black-spotted sunfish; the shellcracker, or red-ear sunfish; the warmouth; and the black crappie, generally known locally as speckled perch.

The bluegill, or "brim" as he's usually called in the South, is easily the most popular of Florida's fresh-water panfish. For that matter, his following among native Florida fresh-water fishermen probably exceeds that of his more glamorous cousin, the largemouth bass. This is surely the case in my home town of Clewiston. When the word spreads that "the brim are beddin'," folks who haven't wet a line for months rush to dress their fly lines or check the rigging on their cane poles. Everyone suddenly becomes very busy digging worms, tying flies, or making leaders. The tackle counters enjoy brisk business, boat rentals at the local fishing camps increase markedly, and the stampede for bluegills is on.

Why are unpretentious bluegills so popular in a fabulous fishing state like Florida? An easy question. They are easy to find, easy to reach, easy to catch, and easy to eat. They are neither snobbish, nor capricious, nor unpredictable. They don't care which way the winds blow, and they pay little attention to the phase of the moon. They are fish of simple tastes and direct purpose, not a bit choosy about how, when, where, or what they eat. Bluegills simply eat whatever they can find whenever they feel hungry ... and they nearly always seem to be hungry!

To discuss all the possible methods of fishing for bluegills would almost require a book devoted to the subject. In Florida, however, only the fly rod and the cane pole are used to any great extent. The bluegill and the light fly rod are more compatible than ham and eggs. The bream's spunky little fight is more pleasing on light fly tackle than on any other type of equipment, and artificial flies will take more and bigger bluegills—day in, day out—than any natural bait. Only during the winter months do Florida bluegills seem to prefer natural bait to artificial flies.

Although bluegills are not particular about fly color or pattern, the fly itself is nevertheless of prime importance to successful fly-fishing for them. The main requisite is that it be small enough to be easily encompassed by the bluegill's tiny mouth. Hooks larger than size 8 simply will not snare a respectable percentage of bluegill strikes, while little size 12's and 14's will make connections nearly every time.

There is no more killing lure for Florida bluegills than a size 14 bivisible dry fly, heavily dressed with a good dry-fly oil or line dressing for better floatability. Dry flies are seldom seen in Florida, and "Cracker" bluegills are easily fooled by them. Dry flies are best late in the evening, when the water surface is slick and insects are on the prowl. Fish them on very light leaders, and don't try to manipulate them too much on the water. Just cast them out, and the bluegills will do the rest. I have yet to meet a native fisherman in Florida who has tried genuine dry flies for bluegills, but I have had many an evening's picnic with these panfish, using a brown bivisible along the shores of Lake Okeechobee's rim canal.

Small cork or plastic popping bugs are highly popular bluegill lures in Florida, and these are indeed hard to beat where bluegills are concerned. Easier to fish than dry flies because they float better, poppers in sizes 8 and 10 will probably catch more bluegills for the average fly fisherman. I have never been able to convince myself that one color is better than another in a bluegill popper, but several Florida tackle dealers tell me that a yellow-and-black bumblebee pattern is their best seller. Poppers should be fished very slowly for best results, with long pauses between pops to give the bluegills time to rise in their leisurely fashion.

During windy or cool weather, wet flies and other sinking lures produce much better than floaters. Among the best of the subsurface lures for Florida bluegills are the sponge-rubber spiders with rubber-band legs. These may be fished dry at the surface, or squeezed between the fingers underwater so that they soak up moisture and sink quickly. A size 8 or 10 spider, in either yellow or black with white legs, really drives bluegills crazy in most Florida waters.

I have had excellent luck with Florida bluegills using ordinary trout-style wet flies and streamers. Most of the bright-colored patterns, like the Royal Coachman, McGinty, Professor, and Yellow Sally, seem to interest bluegills more than the subdued styles, probably because they show up better in the dark waters in which Florida "brim" are apt to be found. I like to fish wet flies with a floating fly line, which serves very well as an indicator for the many strikes that come while the fly is sinking. The slightest twitch of the floating line calls for a quick lift of the rod tip. The retrieve with wet flies should be slow and erratic, gauged so that the fly moves along close to the bottom where the fish are accustomed to looking for aquatic insects and fresh-water shrimp.

If you happen to own an ultra-light fly rod, by all means use it for bluegills in Florida. The ten- and twelve-inchers commonly found in many of Florida's lakes will give you an interesting time on an extra-light outfit. Even medium- or heavyweight rods will give you a lot of fun with Florida bluegills, however, and will come in handy for the occasional lunker bass that may like the looks of your bream flies.

Your fly reel for bluegills and other Florida panfish is strictly a matter of personal choice, since these fish may be played directly from any automatic or single-action reel. The line, however, is very important. The new floating lines like Gladding's Aerofloat or Cortland's 333 will greatly increase your bluegill catch by enabling you to do a better job of fishing either surface or sinking flies.

Leaders at least six feet long, and tapered to about four-pound test on the terminal end, will catch many more bluegills than the short, heavy leaders frequently used for panfishing. Small flies demand the use of long and light leaders, which give the flies better balance on the water and an appearance of being detached from the line.

A pastime enjoyed by a large segment of Florida's population, cane-poling for bluegills, is a wonderful way to relax and a lot of fun to boot. You can buy a good, limber cane pole almost anywhere in Florida for about a dollar, spend another quarter for a small coil of six- or eight-pound-test nylon monofilament, invest a nickel in hooks and another in a small cork bobber, and you're in business. (But don't forget the fishing license unless you're a legal Florida resident and plan to fish in your home county!)

Cut a piece of nylon monofilament about as long as the pole, and tie it securely to the tip. Slip a cork ball float on the line, then tie on a size 8 Carlisle or Eagle Claw hook. As a rule, no sinker is needed, but if it happens to be windy a small split shot above the hook will help to control things for you.

Each section of Florida has its own favorite bluegill bait, with grubs, catalpa worms, live fresh-water shrimp, and cockroaches each considered tops in certain areas. Bluegills are bluegills no matter where you meet them, however, and they all find it hard to resist a lively earthworm. Worms are easy to come by these days; you can buy them by the pint in any Florida tackle store or fresh-water fishing camp.

Light spinning tackle may be used with a plastic bubble or spinning fly line head to cast flies and popping bugs for bluegills, and these fish give a pretty good account of themselves when hooked on light spinning gear. The bubble is easier to cast, but flies may be fished more effectively with a fly line head. Either rig is far inferior to a fly rod. While I have caught lots of Florida bluegills with regular spinning lures, I feel that spinning is a relatively poor fishing method for them. With crappie and warmouth, however, it's another story.

Throughout Florida the black crappie is known generally as speckled perch, or simply "speck." Just to keep the record straight, the crappie is not a perch at all, but a sunfish. Only a sunfish—a relative of the bluegill and black bass—could be so cocky, aggressive, and pugnacious as this fellow. In spite of his swaggering manner and chip-on-the-shoulder attitude, however, the crappie is not a hard fighter. Nevertheless, he's fun to catch, and in the lush feeding conditions of some Florida waters he's apt to be hard enough to fool with artificial lures to make a truly challenging quarry.

I must confess that Florida crappies have snubbed my choicest artificial-lure offerings on many occasions when bait fishermen had no trouble taking them. I used to think that I could catch any panfish on artificial flies if the fish could be caught at all, but Florida crappies have restored my humility. I don't mean to imply that they can never be taken readily with artificials, but only that natural baits are much more dependable. Natural foods are so abundant in many Florida lakes and streams that the crappies can afford to be particular.

The crappie's natural foods in Florida waters are small minnows and fresh-water shrimps, and these are by far the best live baits for crappie fishing. While worms, insects, and small crayfish will occasionally tempt crappie, these baits hardly qualify as mediocre when compared to minnows or shrimp.

The good old cane pole and bobber is unquestionably the most popular rig for crappie fishing in Florida, and this rig can be deadly if a few basic light-tackle principles are incorporated into it. A small hook of light wire, such as a size 8 Sproat, will allow a minnow or shrimp to show considerably more life than would a larger, heavier hook. The bobber should not be too buoyant, or it might arouse the suspicions of light-biting crappies and cause them to drop or tear off the bait before you can hook them. A quill float is best, but a small, slender cork is also satisfactory. No sinker should be used unless strong winds or currents make it necessary to anchor things down a bit. At any rate, shy away from anything heavier than a small split shot.

The best way to hook a minnow for crappies is through the forward part of the eye sockets. With a light-wire hook this can be done without actually piercing the eyeballs, and the skull bones of the minnow serve as reinforcement against the hook's tearing out. Minnows also may be hooked through the lips, the back, or just forward of the tail, but take care not to pierce the backbone or the bait won't live long. The tiny fresh-water shrimps work well either threaded on a very light-weight hook, or hooked through the head just in front of the dark spot.

For the most fun with crappies there's nothing like a light fly rod, although you may have to use live bait on it for positive results at times. Best fly-rod artificials are fly-rod spoons, fly-and-spinner combinations, and streamer flies. I have caught crappies by accident in Lake Okeechobee and other Florida waters on surface bugs while fishing for bass or blue-gills, but surface lures and crappies are generally incompatible.

In fly-fishing for crappies, a slow but active retrieve is a must. Let the lure sink nearly to the bottom, then retrieve with erratic jerks, pausing for several seconds between each jerk. Watch the line closely during the pauses, and if it twitches, sock him! Crappies are light strikers, and you must stay on your toes to hook them consistently.

Spinning is miles ahead of any other artificial-lure fishing method for crappies because it lends itself so well to deep fishing with small lures. Weighted bucktails and streamer flies, small spoons, and many of the European-type spinning lures are excellent for crappies, and all may be fished down deep where the fish usually lie. One of the very best rigs I've tried for crappies with a spinning outfit is an ordinary unweighted streamer fished a foot or two below a size 7 split shot. The unweighted fly has more freedom of action than weighted types, and the crappies really seem to notice the difference.

Just a day or two before this was written I spent a couple of hours on the Fisheating Creek bridge at Lakeport, fishing for crappies and warmouth with spinning tackle. I tried all of my usually reliable lures, but all I could get was one small warmouth. Several fishermen using live minnows appeared to be doing no better than I, so there didn't seem to be much hope for the fried-crappie dinner I'd promised the kids. Before giving up, however, I tied on a little Mickey Finn bucktail and pinched a split shot on the line about two feet above it. My first cast alongside the bridge brought a strike that surprised me so much I forgot to strike back. A couple of casts later, however, I connected with a fat twelve-inch crappie. Working both sides of the bridge thoroughly, I managed to land four more nice specks. Not a big catch, but a satisfying and tasty one, thanks to a size 10 Mickey Finn and split shot.

Crappies are very susceptible to trolled lures, particularly small weighted bucktails like the size 1 or 4 Uppermans. The new, quiet outboard motors are wonderful for this, as they can be throttled down to a noiseless crawl and don't seem to frighten the fish a bit. Harry Sheppard of Pahokee tells me he's been slaying the crappies in Taylor Creek (on the north end of Lake Okeechobee) this way, using trimmed-down Upperman bucktails dyed blue in Rit. Slow trolling is an unbeatable way to locate schools of crappies, even if you intend to cast or still-fish for them after you find them.

The crappie is plentiful in most of Florida's lakes, creeks, and fresh-water rivers, but does not take to the canals like some other panfish or the bass. Most active in the spring and fall, he strikes fairly well in winter, but only sporadically during the summer months.

Look for crappies around fallen trees, lily pads, bridges—or for that matter, any sort of cover—in water four or more feet deep. In creeks, give attention to bends where the banks are cut deep, and to the mouths of branch streams and coves. If you want to be sure of finding Florida crappies in a striking mood, look for them in March or April.

Another of Florida's highly popular panfish is the warmouth, a fish closely related to and superficially resembling the rock bass of the more northern states. A ready striker, the warmouth is easily fooled by almost any sort of small artificial lure. Like his cousin, the rock bass, the warmouth hits hard, but gives up rather quickly when hooked. He's fun to catch, however, and makes fine eating.

The best tackle for warmouths is the lightest of spinning gear, for these fish really go for tiny spinning lures in the one-tenth-ounce class. My favorite warmouth lure is a homemade creation I call an "Owl-Eye," made by pinching a size 5 split shot on a size 4 hook just behind the eye, painting the shot yellow or white, and tying a short length of bucktail behind the shot. My early models of this lure were decorated with big round eyes on the head, but the fish seem to like it just as well without the eyes. Other good spinning lures for warmouth are the number 4 Upperman bucktail, the size 4 No-Alibi jig, and the Crimson Dart. All of these jig-type lures should be bounced right along the bottom for warmouths, and when fished in this manner they will take fish when everything else—including natural bait—fails. Spinning is especially effective for warmouth during the fall and winter months when the fish are deep.

Florida warmouths, like bluegills, do a lot of surface feeding in the spring and summer, and during these seasons they are easily caught by fly-fishing. Warmouths will hit any of the surface flies recommended for bluegills, and are frequently taken as well on bass-size bugs and poppers. Generally speaking, however, small streamer flies will tempt more warmouths than any other lures for the fly rod.

The warmouth is one of the most cannibalistic of the pan-sized sunfishes, and any small minnow will make good natural bait for him. He'll also bite worms, grasshoppers, live or dead shrimp, and nearly anything else that happens to get in his way when he's hungry. Whatever the natural bait, fish it very close to the bottom if you want warmouths.

Warmouths may be found over mud or weedy bottom in just about any Florida pond, stream, or canal. They love to hang around cypress knees, logs, bridges, or other cover in water from four to six feet deep. Give particular attention to the old wooden bridges spanning many of Florida's creeks and canals, for if there's one hangout the warmouth dearly loves, it's an old wooden bridge.

As mentioned earlier, several other important sunfishes are common in Florida waters. The shellcracker is the largest, reaching about the same size as the bluegill. This fish gets its name from its habit of feeding on small snails, cracking their shells in its small but powerful jaws. Shellcrackers prefer clear, sand-bottomed lakes to streams or canals. They strike the same lures and natural baits as bluegills, but are somewhat less vulnerable to surface lures. The red-edged gill flap is a fairly reliable means of identification for this species.

Another Florida sunfish, the stumpknocker, likes to hang around cypress knees and pick off bugs that crawl down to the water line. This action produces a noise that sounds like a fish knocking on a stump; hence the name stumpknocker. Essentially a stream fish, he is also found in canals and some lakes. He, too, sees eye to eye with the bluegill on the question of artificial lures and natural bait. A small popper cast right up against a cypress knee is nearly always more than he can resist. Stumpknockers are most numerous in the creeks and rivers of the West Florida panhandle, but are distributed throughout most of the state. The numerous black spots running in horizontal rows along the body, and the relatively large mouth, will serve to identify this sunfish.

The red-breast is a familiar panfish to fresh-water fishermen along the entire Eastern seaboard. He ranges throughout Florida as well, and is fairly common in most of the fast-flowing streams in the state, occurring in greatest numbers in the St. John's River and its tributaries. The red-breast will usually hit any small fly without hesitation . . . but in case he does hesitate, feed him a worm. You can identify the red-breast by —you guessed it—his red breast. The long gill flap confirms the identification.

Here's one last little tip on a weakness common to all of Florida's panfish. They are nuts about pork rind. For crappies or warmouth, try a small fly-rod spinner with an inch or so of pork strip trailing behind it. Fish it with an up-and-down motion, so that the spinner flutters as it sinks and spins as it is raised. The flash of the spinner calls the fish to attention, and the tantalizing wiggle of the pork rind clinches the deal.

For bluegills, shellcrackers, and the other Florida sunfish, try a one-half- to three-fourths-inch sliver of thin pork rind on a size 10 hook. This is best fished with a fly rod in the same manner you'd fish a wet fly; that is, slowly and erratically.

You can't beg, borrow, steal, or buy a better underwater lure for sunfish.

That about covers the fresh-water panfish of Florida, although in a literal sense the term "panfish" might very well be applied to the fresh-water catfishes, which are numerous throughout the state. In the pan, catfish are certainly hard to beat. Channel and blue cats are found in every Florida river, and every canal, lake, and creek contains plenty of speckled and yellow bullheads. If you do any cane-poling for panfish in Florida, you're bound to catch a few catfish. The speckled bullhead is probably the most common species, and he's the fellow who sparks the famous dish of "catfish and hush puppies." Catfish are easily caught at any season of the year in Florida, on the same baits they like the country over.

CHAPTER **16**

Summary and Suggestions

A FISHERMAN visiting Florida for the first time feels like a little boy turned loose in a candy factory; he hardly knows where to start. The total salt-water shore line, including all island shores and indentations, measures over 8,000 miles,[1] and the inland area of the state is about one-twelfth fresh water. The combined shore lines of the fresh water lakes alone total over 25,000 miles. Where to start indeed!

Actually, the problem isn't so great as it might seem, for all sections of Florida contribute to the state's reputation as a fisherman's paradise. Where to go depends on when you make your trip, what kind of fishing you want, how much you want to spend, and perhaps to some extent on how far you want to

---

[1] If you think this figure is an exaggeration, fly over the Ten Thousand Islands sections of Florida's lower west coast some time. There's many a mile of island shore line right here—so much, in fact, that the 8,000 figure seems conservative.

206

drive. For example, if you drive from some Midwestern point and enter Florida near Pensacola, you'll still have over 800 miles to go to try the fishing around Key West. You may not care to sacrifice the precious vacation time these 800-odd extra miles of driving would require, and if this is the case, you'd best forget the Keys and try some of the exceptional fishing along the Gulf coast from Pensacola to St. Marks. On the other hand, if you want to catch bonefish, you'll have to travel at least as far south as Miami, and preferably all the way down to the Keys.

Then there's the matter of the season of the year. North Florida, unfortunately, gets a bit chilly from time to time during the winter months, and many of the fish move farther south. For this reason, many of the fishing spots in Northwest Florida close from December until March or April, and the camp and charter-boat operators either take a vacation or set up shop in a more southerly location. For example, my good friend Roy Martin, manager of the Panama City Beach fishing pier and holder of many world game fish records, takes over his tackle shop at the huge Key Colony Motel down in Marathon when winter arrives. Come spring, and Roy hurries back to Panama City Beach in time for the hot fishing the warm weather brings.

In wintertime, the salt-water fishing improves as you go south, reaching its peak in the Keys. In spring, summer, and fall, however, salt-water fishing is just as good in North and West Florida as it is in the southern part of the state—and sometimes better.

When the question of how much Florida fishing will cost arises, the answer can range from nothing to over $100 a day. The bridges, jetties, beaches, and many of the piers on the

Gulf and east coasts are free. Not even a license is required of either resident or nonresident salt-water fishermen.

Skiff rentals will range from a ridiculously low $1.00 per day on some inland waters to $1.50 or $2.00 per day on the Gulf coast, and up to $5.00 daily on the lower east coast and Keys. The over-all average skiff-rental rate in Florida wouldn't be much over $2.00. For these inflated times, that's a steal. Skiffs with outboard motors rent at rates of from $8.00 to $12.00 a day, including enough gasoline for the day's fishing. Rental outboards take a dreadful beating and are sometimes unreliable. For this reason, I strongly recommend that you bring your own kicker when you take that Florida vacation. You'll save money, and perhaps a lot of headaches. While some Florida fishing camps keep their rental motors in good shape, the majority, I'm sorry to say, do not.

Bottom-fishing party boats accommodating as many as fifty eager fishermen operate in the more populous areas such as Miami, Tampa, and Jacksonville. The cost runs from $3.00 to $5.00 per person for a day's fishing, and this usually includes bait . . . and, in some cases, tackle. No reservation is necessary; just be at the dock on time. (Usually 8:00 or 9:00 A.M.) Party-boat trips are a good bet for the casual fishermen, and they nearly always get plenty of fish.

Charter boats that work the Gulf Stream out of east coast ports charge from $40 to $100 per day, depending on season and location. Summer rates are lower than the rates charged during the tourist season. Tackle is supplied, but most skippers have no objection to anglers' using their own.

Gulf Stream charter boats troll for sailfish, marlin, wahoo, dolphin, and kingfish, with sailfish the principal quarry. If you want to catch a Florida sailfish, you'll have to make a charter trip into the Gulf Stream. The entire lower east coast of Florida is productive of sailfish, but if you want to be reasonably certain of getting one, fish out of Stuart or Palm Beach in January.

While the rates for Gulf Stream fishing seem high, they aren't really too bad when four fishermen split the cost. And when you consider the high initial investment, expensive upkeep and dock space, and the relatively short duration of the "season," it makes you wonder how the charter-boat skippers get along on what they charge.

Gulf Coast charter boatmen specialize in tarpon fishing during the spring and summer, and offshore trolling for kingfish (king mackerel) in fall and winter. Their rates, generally, are lower than those on Florida's "Gold Coast," seldom exceeding $50 for a day's fishing. Reservations for charter-boat fishing should always be made well in advance, especially during the tourist or tarpon seasons. (The tourist season occurs in summer, remember, in North Florida.)

There are plenty of native fishing guides in most sections of Florida, and most of them do a good job of finding fish for their clients. Their services may cost a mere $8.00 a day for bass fishing in North Florida, or as high as $50 daily (including boat and motor) for bonefishing in the Keys. If you can afford a guide, by all means hire one. Most of them are full of colorful Cracker talk and interesting stories, and they usually can find the fish for you. Guides do all the work of loading and unloading the boat, handling the oars, and running the outboard. They really earn whatever fee they charge.

Eating and sleeping accommodations for the touring fisherman in Florida are not too bad if you steer clear of such show places as Miami Beach during the busy winter season.

Motel rates vary with the season from an average considerably below that of the country as a whole during slack periods to higher than the national average when the "No Vacancy" signs prevail. In general, there is less variation in rates from month to month on the Gulf coast and around the smaller towns of interior Florida.

Florida's fresh-water fishing regulations are liberalized, no closed seasons being observed throughout most of the state. Certain waters in Calhoun, Gulf, and Jackson Counties are closed to all fishing during the months of April and May, but all other fresh waters are open the year round.

The daily bag limit is twenty-five fresh-water fish per person, no more than eight of which may be bass. Rough fish, of course, are not included as part of the limit, but it is important to note that the figure of twenty-five applies to the sum total of game and panfish, and not twenty-five of each species. There is no size limit on any fresh-water fish; anything you want to keep is a keeper.

License fees are $2.00 annually for resident anglers, $10.50 annually for nonresidents, and $3.25 for nonresident fourteen-day permits. Annual licenses run on the fiscal year of July 1 through June 30. Residents under 15 and over 65 years of age may fish without a license, and service men stationed in Florida are accorded resident license privileges. Legal Florida residents are still permitted to fish the waters of their home counties with cane poles without buying a fishing license. Perhaps some day the state legislature will see the light and make the cane-polers pay their fair share toward the management of fresh-water fisheries, but up to now, at least, this issue has been too hot a political potato for the vote-conscious legislators to handle.

When you buy your Florida fishing license, be sure to get the folder summarizing the fishing rules and regulations. The laws may change slightly from time to time, and you'll want to be up to date. Specific regulations on the use of motorboats in certain lakes are given, as are the specific waters observing closed fishing seasons.

No license is required of the salt-water fisherman in Florida, unless he intends to sell his catch. Resident anglers are permitted to sell their fish to a licensed wholesaler without paying a fee, but the nonresident must buy a commercial fisherman's license (fee, $25.00) to do this. Residents and nonresidents alike are required to purchase a license to operate their pleasure boats when the combined length and beam total more than twenty feet. This fee amounts to $1.25 for a twenty-one-footer, and $.20 additional per foot thereafter.

Tarpon and sailfish are rigidly protected in Florida, the bag limit being two per person per day. It is illegal to sell tarpon or sailfish, although enforcement is lax in some eastcoast areas where smoked sailfish flesh is peddled openly.

Certain other salt-water game and food fish enjoy size-limit privileges. While these minimum legal lengths were established mainly to apply to the catch of commercial fishermen, they do apply as well to that of the angler. The game fish involved and their minimum legal lengths are: Bluefish, 10 inches; mackerel, 12 inches; sea trout, 12 inches; snook, 18 inches; pompano, 10 inches; and redfish (channel bass), 15 inches. Lengths are measured from the tip of the jaw to the fork of the tail.

That about sums up the rules and regulations that concern the Florida sports fisherman. While there are closed seasons on mullet and shad, the average angler is little affected.

Provision is made for bait-dealers to handle mullet during the closed season, and the closed shad season comes when the run is about over anyway.

The Florida Game and Fresh Water Fish Commission at Tallahassee will send you free upon request a booklet called *Fishing Florida's Fresh Waters*. It contains a brief run-down on each of Florida's fresh-water game fish, and a county-by-county directory of fresh-water fishing camps. This directory of fishing camps should prove of great value to the visiting fisherman, or to the vacationing Floridian who wants to explore the fishing in some other part of the state. Information is given on the number of boats available, number of cabins, if any, and the body of water on which each camp is located.

To everyone sufficiently interested in Florida fishing to have read this far, I strongly recommend *Florida Wildlife* magazine, the monthly publication of the Game and Fresh Water Fish Commission. Subscriptions may be ordered at $2.00 per year—from *Florida Wildlife*, Game and Fresh Water Fish Commission, Tallahassee. It is a slick magazine, beautifully illustrated, and full of informative reading about outdoor Florida. Many of the stories are authored by well-known and highly regarded names in the field of outdoor writing. Stories on both fresh- and salt-water fishing appear in its pages.

The Florida State Board of Conservation, which regulates salt-water fishing, publishes an attractive booklet of interest to the salt-water angler. Titled *Florida Salt Water Fishing*, it is available free for the asking from the Board of Conservation, Tallahassee. Excellent illustrations of most of the fish mentioned in this book are included, along with a number of mouth-watering recipes for Florida seafood cookery. For a three cent stamp or a postcard, this booklet is a whale of a bargain.

Every fisherman visiting Florida should make an effort to spend a day at Marine Studios, located between St. Augustine and Daytona Beach on Route A1A. There, through the portholes of the Oceanarium, you can see specimens of many of the fish you'll be catching, and you can see them in their natural environment. Well-informed and courteous guides at Marine Studios will explain the habits of the different fish to you or answer any questions you may have. To a fisherman, a visit to this fantastic Oceanarium is a must, the greatest of the many great tourist attractions in Florida.

The State of Florida may appear to some as a crazy conglomeration of gaudy carnivals, with pitchmen and barkers trying to get the tourist's buck from one end of the peninsula to the other. Steve Trumbull, the Miami Herald roving reporter, has called it "the world's longest midway." To a fisherman, however, Florida is more than a midway. It's paradise, surrounded by motels and hotels and race tracks and fruit stands, all of which cease to exist when it's time to go fishing. The real Florida, the fisherman's Florida, is still relatively unspoiled by the gaudy veneer of the "Gold Coast." It is still the nearest thing to a fisherman's heaven you can find without leaving the United States. I hope this book will help you find the kind of fishing Florida can offer. And I hope, too, that at least some of your big ones don't get away.

_____

Common Anglers' Fishes of Florida

The standard common names of the fish listed are those accepted by the Outdoor Writers Association of America, while the scientific names have the approval of both the OWAA and the American Fisheries Society. Also given are the names of the fish as commonly used in Florida, for in many cases local nomenclature differs from the standard.

The range of the fish is given from a practical standpoint and is limited to those areas in which the fish are reasonably certain to be found. For example, bonefish have been taken as far north as Sebastian Inlet, but for all practical purposes they do not range north of Miami.

The good spots as given for each fish are not necessarily the best spots, nor are they the only good spots in most cases. They are places known to be productive of the fish for which they are listed.

SALT-WATER FISH

STANDARD NAME	COMMON FLORIDA NAMES	RANGE	SEASON	ABUNDANCE	GOOD SPOTS
AMBERJACK (*Seriola dumerili*)	Same	Offshore, entire Florida coast, over reefs	All year in Keys; spring & summer elsewhere	Common	Panama City Beach; Key Largo
BARRACUDA, GREAT (*Sphyraena barracuda*)	Same; 'cuda	Ft. Pierce to Key West, inshore and offshore	All year; spring and fall best	Plentiful	Keys
BASS, CHANNEL (*Sciaenops ocellatus*)	Redfish	Bay of Florida to Pensacola on Gulf coast; Miami north	All year, fall best	Plentiful	Upper east coast; 10,000 Islands; Pine Island area
BASS, SEA (*Centropristes striatus*)	Same	Offshore, Fernandina to Melbourne; Sanibel to Pensacola	Fall and winter best	Not common	Offshore, upper east coast
BASS, STRIPED (*Roccus saxatilis*)	Same	St. Johns River from Jacksonville to Lake George	Fall and winter best	Not numerous	St. Johns River
BLUEFISH (*Pomatomus saltatrix*)	Same	Entire Florida coast line, offshore, in surf, and in bays	Spring, fall and winter	Common to plentiful	Ft. Pierce to Boca Raton
BONEFISH (*Albula vulpes*)	Same	Miami south to Key West over shallow flats	All year	Common to plentiful	Key Largo; Islamorada

216

STANDARD NAME	COMMON FLORIDA NAMES	RANGE	SEASON	ABUNDANCE	GOOD SPOTS
BONITO, ATLANTIC (*Sarda sarda*)	Bonito	Offshore, entire Florida coast	All year, winter best	Common	Off Palm Beach
BONITO, OCEANIC (*Katsuwonus vagans*)	Arctic Bonito	Edge of Gulf Stream from Ft. Pierce to Key West	Spring and summer	Fairly common; not plentiful	Gulf Stream off Keys
CATFISH, GAFFTOPSAIL (*Bagre marinus*)	Sail Cat	Tampa Bay south to 10,000 Islands. Bays and open Gulf	All year, summer best	Plentiful	San Carlos Bay area
COBIA (*Rachycentron canadus*)	Same; Cabio; Ling	Off shore, entire Florida coast. Channels in bays of Gulf coast	Spring through fall, west coast. Fall and winter, lower east coast	Common on Gulf coast	Panama City; Cedar Keys; San Carlos Bay area
CROAKER (*Micropogon undulatus*)	Same	Fernandina to Miami on east coast. Pensacola to Tampa Bay on Gulf coast. Surf and bays	All year	Common	Bays and surf, Fernandina to Daytona Beach
CUTLASSFISH (*Trichiurus lepturnus*)	Ribbon-fish	Bays of east coast south to Miami	All year	Fairly common	St. Lucie Inlet
DOLPHIN (*Coryphaena bipparus*)	Same	Off shore in blue water, entire Florida coast	All year	Plentiful	Gulf Stream, Palm Beach through Keys

217

SALT-WATER FISH

STANDARD NAME	COMMON FLORIDA NAMES	RANGE	SEASON	ABUNDANCE	GOOD SPOTS
DRUM, BLACK (*Pogonias cromis*)	Same	Inlets, bays, surf; entire coast north of Keys	All year	Common	St. Augustine area
FLOUNDER, SOUTHERN (*Paralichthys lethostigmus*)	Same	Bays and surf of entire Florida coast	All year	Common to plentiful	Panama City; upper east coast
GROUPER, BLACK (*Mycteropeoca bonaci*)	Same	Reefs off shore, entire Florida coast. Spotty on east coast north of Miami	All year	Uncommon to plentiful	Off Keys; off Tampa Bay
GROUPER, CONEY (*Cephalopholis fulvus*)	Coney	Deep reefs off Keys	All year	Rare	Off Marathon
GROUPER, GAG (*Mycteroperca microleris*)	Gag; Black Grouper	Bays and offshore reefs from Tampa Bay and Ft. Pierce south	All year	Uncommon to plentiful	Tampa Bay; San Carlos Bay; Key Largo
GROUPER, NASSAU (*Epinephelus striatus*)	Same	Entire east coast; north to Tampa bay on west coast	All year	Common	Keys reefs
GROUPER, RED (*Epinephelus morio*)	Same	Reefs and rocky bottom off entire Florida coast	All year	Plentiful	Banks off Pensacola; Keys reefs

218

STANDARD NAME	COMMON FLORIDA NAMES	RANGE	SEASON	ABUNDANCE	GOOD SPOTS
GROUPER, RED HIND (*Epinephelus guttatus*)	Red Hind	Deeper reefs, Key Largo to Key West	All year	Not abundant	Alligator Reef (off Islamorada)
GROUPER, ROCKHIND (*Epinephelus adsensionis*)	Rock-hind	Deep reefs, Miami to Key West	All year	Common	Outer reefs off Keys
GROUPER, YELLOWFIN (*Mycteroperca venenosa*)	Same	Outer reefs, Miami to Key West	All year	Not common	Reefs off lower Keys
GRUNT, BLACK MARGATE (*Anisotremus surinaminsis*)	Same; Pom-pom	Hard bottom, Palm Beach to Key West, inshore and off shore	All year	Common	Lower Keys
GRUNT, BLUE STRIPED (*Haemulon sciurus*)	Same; Blue Grunt	Hard bottom, Palm Beach to Key West	All year	Common	Keys
GRUNT, FRENCH (*Haemulon flavolineatum*)	Same; Yellow Grunt	Miami to Key West on rocky bottom	All year	Fairly common	Keys
GRUNT, GRAY (*Haemulon macrostomum*)	Same	Inner and outer reefs, Palm Beach to Key West	All year	Fairly common	Marathon to Key West

SALT-WATER FISH

STANDARD NAME	COMMON FLORIDA NAMES	RANGE	SEASON	ABUNDANCE	GOOD SPOTS
GRUNT, MARGATE (Haemulon album)	Margot; Margate	Reefs and rocky inlets, Miami to Key West	All year	Common	Upper Key Largo
GRUNT, WHITE (Haemulon plumieri)	Same	Ft. Pierce through Keys; bays and reefs	All year	Plentiful	Reefs off Keys
HOUNDFISH (Strongylura raphidoma)	Same	Reefs, bays, Miami to Key West	All year	Common	Reefs off Keys
JACK, CREVALLE (Caranx hippos)	Jack; Jackfish	Bays, surf, reefs of entire coast	All year	Plentiful	West coast, Tampa Bay to 10,000 Islands
JACK, HORSE-EYE (Caranx latus)	Same	Reefs and edge of Gulf Stream, Stuart to Key West	All year, spring best	Not common	Lower Keys
JACK, YELLOW (Caranx bartholomaei)	Bar Jack	Reefs, St. Lucie Inlet to Key West	All year	Common	Off Key Largo
JEWFISH, BLACK (Garrupa nigrita)	Warsaw Grouper	Very deep off-shore reefs, entire Florida coast	All year	Common	Off Panama City, off Miami
JEWFISH, SPOTTED (Promicrops itaiara)	Jewfish	Entire coast line, inshore and off-shore reefs, bridges, creeks	All year, summer best	Common	Boca Grande Pass, 10,000 Islands, reefs off Keys

220

STANDARD NAME	COMMON FLORIDA NAMES	RANGE	SEASON	ABUNDANCE	GOOD SPOTS
LADYFISH (*Elops saurus*)	Same; Chiro	Bays, surf, inlets of entire Florida coast	All year, summer best	Plentiful	Boca Grande to 10,000 Islands
LIZZARDFISH (*Synodus foetens*)	Same; Cigarfish	Inshore over entire coast	All year	Common	Charlotte Harbor
LOOKDOWN (*Selene vomer*)	Moonfish	Bridges and jetties, St. Lucie Inlet to Key West	All year	Common	Keys bridges
MACKEREL, CERO (*Scomberomorus regalis*)	Same	Reefs, Miami to Key West	Late winter through fall	Common	Reefs off Keys
MACKEREL, KING (*Scomberomorus cavalla*)	Kingfish	Off shore, entire Florida coast	All year, spring and fall best	Plentiful	Off Naples, lower east coast
MACKEREL, SPANISH (*Scomberomorus maculatus*)	Same	Bays, inlets, inshore reefs of entire coast	All year, spring and fall best	Plentiful	Naples, Palm Beach
MARLIN, BLUE, (*Makaira nigricans ampla*)	Same	East edge of Gulf Stream, Ft. Pierce south	Spring and summer	Rare	East side of Gulf Stream, Palm Beach to Key Largo
MARLIN, WHITE (*Makaira albida*)	Same	Gulf Stream off entire east coast	January to June	Fairly common; not abundant	Palm Beach to Ft. Lauderdale
MULLET (*Mugil cephalus*)	Same	Surf, bays, rivers of entire Florida coast	All year	Plentiful	Bays of west coast

SALT-WATER FISH

STANDARD NAME	COMMON FLORIDA NAMES	RANGE	SEASON	ABUNDANCE	GOOD SPOTS
PALOMETA (*Trachinotus glaucus*)	Pompano	Surf, Melbourne to Miami; also deeper flats in Keys	Spring and summer	Not common	Natural channels in Keys
PERMIT (*Trachinotus goodei*)	Same; Mexican Pompano	Tampa Bay, south to 10,000 Islands. Ft. Pierce, south through Keys	All year, summer best	Not abundant	Boca Grande Pass, Content Keys
PIGFISH (*Orthopristis chrysopterus*)	Same	Bays of entire Florida coast line	All year	Common to plentiful	Tampa Bay, San Carlos Bay
PINFISH (*Lagodon rhomboides*)	Same; Sailor's choice	Grassy bays of entire Florida coast line	All year	Plentiful	Sarasota Bay
POMPANO (*Trachinotus carolinus*)	Same	Surf, bays, inlets of entire coast	All year, spring best	Common to plentiful	Sarasota Bay, Biscayne Bay, Juno Beach
POMPANO, AFRICAN (*Hynnis cubensis*)	Same; Cuban Jack	Outer reefs, Miami to Key West	Early spring through summer	Not common	Outer reefs off Key Largo
POMPANO, ROUND (*Trachinotus falcattus*)	Same	Southern halves of both coasts	Summer best	Not common	Beaches, Naples to Ft. Myers
PORGY, GRASS (*Calamus arctifrons*)	Same	Grassy bottom in bays of west coast	All year	Fairly common	Tampa Bay

222

STANDARD NAME	COMMON FLORIDA NAMES	RANGE	SEASON	ABUNDANCE	GOOD SPOTS
PORGY, JOLTHEAD (*Calamus bajonado*)	Same	Ocean bottom, Palm Beach to Key West	All year	Fairly common	Hard sandy bottom off Keys
PORGY, LITTLEHEAD (*Calamus proridens*)	Same	Same as Jolthead Porgy	All year	Fairly common	Same as Jolthead
PORGY, SOUTHERN (*Stenotomus aculeatus*)	Porgy	Hard bottom inshore and off shore, entire coast	All year	Fairly common	Fernandina to St. Augustine
PORKFISH (*Anistoremus virginicus*)	Same	Rocky bottom, Tampa Bay south through Keys and up to Ft. Pierce	All year	Common	Reefs off Keys
RUNNER (*Caranx ruber*)	Blue Runner	Over reers and hard bottom, Ft. Pierce to Key West	All year	Common	Reefs off Keys
RUNNER, BLUE (*Caranx cripos*)	Same	Bays, inlets, and off shore, entire Florida coast	All year	Plentiful	Keys, beaches of lower east coast
RUNNER, RAINBOW (*Elagatis bipinnulatus*)	Same	Outer reefs and Gulf Stream, Miami to Key West	Summer	Not common	Gulf Stream off Elbow Reef (Key Largo)

223

SALT-WATER FISH

STANDARD NAME	COMMON FLORIDA NAMES	RANGE	SEASON	ABUNDANCE	GOOD SPOTS
SANDFISH (*Diplectrum formosum*)	Sand Perch	Inshore waters of entire coast	All year	Common to plentiful	Biscayne Bay, San Carlos Bay
SAILFISH, ATLANTIC (*Istiophorus americanus*)	Same	Far off shore, west coast; edge of Gulf Stream, east coast	All year	Common to plentiful	Gulf Stream, St. Lucie to Palm Beach Inlets
SAILOR'S CHOICE (*Haemulon parra*)	Same	Palm Beach to Key West over hard bottom	All year	Common	Middle Keys
SEA CATFISH (*Galeichthys felis*)	Same	Bays of entire coast	All year	Plentiful	10,000 Islands north to Tampa Bay
SEA TROUT (or WEAKFISH) (*Cynoscion regalis*)	Same	Bays and inlets, Fernandina to Cocoa	All year	Not common	Fernandina
SEA TROUT, SAND (or SAND WEAKFISH) (*Cynoscion arenarius*)	Gray Trout	Bays of Gulf coast, 10,000 Islands northward	All year, spring best	Common	Boca Grande to San Carlos Bay
SEA TROUT, SILVER (or SILVER WEAKFISH) (*Cynoscion arenarius*)	Silver Trout	Sandy beaches and inlets of Gulf coast	All year, spring and summer best	Fairly common	Panama City Beach
SEA TROUT, SPOTTED (or SPOTTED WEAKFISH)	Speckled Trout	Bays, inlets, and rivers of entire coast line	All year	Plentiful	Pine Island Sound, Tampa Bay

224

STANDARD NAME	COMMON FLORIDA NAMES	RANGE	SEASON	ABUNDANCE	GOOD SPOTS
SHAD (*Alosa sapidissima*)	Same	St. Johns River	December through February	Common	Lemon Bluff
SHEEPSHEAD (*Archosargus probatocephalus*)	Same	Oyster bottoms, pilings, bridges of entire coast	All year	Common to plentiful	Naples to Tampa Bay
SNAPPER, DOG (*Lutjanus jocu*)	Same	Key Largo to Key West, deep and shallow reefs	All year	Not common	Reefs off Key West
SNAPPER, LANE (*Lutjanus synagris*)	Same	St. Lucie Inlet south to Key West, and north to Tampa Bay on Gulf	All year	Common	Channels around lower Keys
SNAPPER, MANGROVE (*Lutjanus griseus*)	Same; Red Snapper; Gray Snapper	Bays, creeks and reefs of entire coast, most numerous in southern half of the state	All year	Plentiful	10,000 Islands, Keys
SNAPPER, MUTTON (*Lutjanus analis*)	Mutton-fish	Offshore reefs of entire east coast, most numerous south of Ft. Pierce	All year, spring best	Uncommon to plentiful	Reefs off Keys
SNAPPER, RED (*Lutjanus aya*)	Same; Pensacola Snapper	Deep water in Gulf; off shore, St. Augustine to Fernandina	All year	Plentiful	Deep, offshore banks, Pensacola to Panama City

225

SALT-WATER FISH

STANDARD NAME	COMMON FLORIDA NAMES	RANGE	SEASON	ABUNDANCE	GOOD SPOTS
SNAPPER, SCHOOLMASTER (*Lutjanus apodus*)	Same	Miami through Keys and in 10,000 Islands	All year	Common	Channels and reefs, lower Keys
SNAPPER, YELLOWTAIL (*Ocyurus chrysurus*)	Yellowtail	St. Lucie Inlet south through Keys, over reefs and rock patches	All year	Common to plentiful	Coral reefs along Keys
SNOOK (*Centropomus undecimalis*)	Same	Bays, creeks, rivers, surf, and inlets, Sebastian Inlet southward through Keys and over entire Gulf coast	All year, summer best	Uncommon to plentiful	10,000 Islands, rivers of lower Gulf coast
SNOOK, FAT (*Centropomus parallelus*)	Same	Bays and inlets, Ft. Pierce south through Keys and 10,000 Islands	All year, summer best	Common	St. Lucie Inlet, St. Lucie River
TARPON (*Tarpon atlanticus*)	Same	Bays, inlets, rivers of entire coast line	All year in southern Florida, summer best	Plentiful	10,000 Islands, Boca Grande Pass, lower Keys
TRIGGERFISH (*Balistes carolinensis*)	Same	Reefs, inlets, pilings over entire coast line	All year, summer best	Common	Keys reefs

226

STANDARD NAME	COMMON FLORIDA NAMES	RANGE	SEASON	ABUNDANCE	GOOD SPOTS
TRIPLETAIL (*Lobotes surinamensis*)	Same; Chobie; Black Perch	Wrecks, pilings, buoys over entire coast	All year, summer best	Rare to common	St. Augustine to Cape Canaveral
TUNA, LITTLE (*Eurthynnus alletteratttus*)	Bonito; False Albacore	Offshore over entire coast	All year, spring and summer best	Common to plentiful	Edge of Gulf Stream, St. Lucie Inlet to Key Largo
TUNA, BLACKFIN (*Parathunnus atlanticus*)	Albacore	Gulf Stream off entire east coast	February through summer	Uncommon	Gulf Stream off Key Largo
TUNA, YELLOWFIN (*Neothunnus argentivittatus*)	Allison Tuna	Miami to Key West, well off shore	January through June	Relatively rare	Gulf Stream off Keys
WAHOO (*Acanthocybium solandri*)	Same	Edge of Gulf Stream, Ft. Pierce through Keys	February through June	Uncommon	Gulf Stream off Ft. Lauderdale
WHITING, SOUTHERN (*Menticirrbus americanus*)	Same	Beaches of east coast south to Miami, straggling to Gulf coast	All year, spring best	Common to plentiful	Surf at Juno Beach
WHITING, SILVER (*Menticirrbus littoralis*)	Same; Gulf Whiting	Beaches of Gulf coast from 10,000 Islands northward	All year, spring best	Common to plentiful	Bonita Beach, Sanibel Island

227

FRESH-WATER FISH

STANDARD NAME	COMMON FLORIDA NAME	RANGE	SEASONS[1]	ABUNDANCE	GOOD SPOTS
BASS, FLORIDA LARGEMOUTH (*Micropterus salmoides floridanus*)	Bass; Trout	All fresh waters of state	All year; spring and fall best	Plentiful	Most lakes and rivers
BASS, LARGEMOUTH (*Micropterus salmoides*)	Bass; Trout	Most fresh waters of state	All year	Plentiful	St. Johns River, north Florida lakes
BASS, SPOTTED (*Micropterus punctulatus*)	Same; Trout	Flint and Chattahoochee Rivers	All year	Relatively rare	Flint River
BASS, SUWANNEE (*Micropterus notius*)	Same; Trout	Suwannee River and its tributaries	All year	Fairly common	Suwannee River
BOWFIN (*Amia calva*)	Mudfish	All fresh waters of state	All year	Common	Canals of South Florida
BLUEGILL (*Lepomis macrochirus*)	Same; Bream	All fresh waters of state	All year, spring and summer best	Plentiful	Lake Okeechobee, north Florida lakes
BULLHEAD, BROWN (*Ameiurus nebulosus*)	Speckled Catfish	Most fresh waters of state	All year	Common to plentiful	Mud-bottomed lakes and streams
BULLHEAD, YELLOW (*Ameiurus natalis*)	Yellow Catfish	Most slow-moving streams of state	All year	Common	Kissimmee River

228

STANDARD NAME	COMMON FLORIDA NAME	RANGE	SEASONS[1]	ABUNDANCE	GOOD SPOTS
CATFISH, CHANNEL (*Ictalurus punctatus*)	Same	Most fresh-water rivers and large streams	All year	Common	Larger rivers of state
CATFISH, WHITE (*Ictalurus catus*)	Same; Channel Cat	Same as Channel Catfish	All year	Common	Larger rivers of state
CRAPPIE, BLACK (*Pomoxis nigromaculatus*)	Speckled Perch	Most lakes and streams of state	All year, spring and fall best	Plentiful	Kissimmee River, central Florida lakes
GAR, ALLIGATOR (*Lepisosteus spatula*)	Same	Fresh waters of West Florida panhandle	All year, summer best	Common	
GAR, LONGNOSED (*Lepisosteus osseus*)	Same; Gator Gar	Most fresh waters of state	All year	Plentiful	Rivers flowing into Gulf of Mexico
GAR, SHORTNOSED (*Lepisosteus platostomus*)	Gar	Most fresh waters of state	All year	Plentiful	Canals of Everglades
GAR, SPOTTED (*Lepisosteus productus*)	Gar	Most fresh waters of state	All year	Plentiful	Canals of Everglades
PICKEREL, CHAIN (*Esox niger*)	Same; Pike; Jackfish	Most weedy fresh waters of state	All year	Rare to common	Dead Lakes, Lake Okeechobee

FRESH-WATER FISH

STANDARD NAME	COMMON FLORIDA NAME	RANGE	SEASONS[1]	ABUNDANCE	GOOD SPOTS
SHINER, GOLDEN (*Notemigonus crysoleucas*)	Shiner	Most weedy fresh waters of state	All year	Plentiful	Lakes of north central Florida
SUNFISH, SPOTTED (*Lepomis punctatus*)	Stump-knocker	Most fresh waters of state, particularly streams and rivers	All year, spring and summer best	Common to plentiful	Streams of West Florida panhandle
SUNFISH, REDBREAST (*Lepomis auritus*)	Redbreast	Most streams throughout the state	All year, spring best	Common to plentiful	St. Johns River
SUNFISH, REDEAR (*Lepomis microlophus*)	Shell-cracker	Clear lakes and streams throughout the state	Spring through fall	Common to plentiful	Lake Okeechobee, Dead Lakes
WARMOUTH (*Chaenobryttus coronarius*)	War-mouth Perch	Lakes and slow-moving streams through the state	All year	Plentiful	Canals and creeks of South Florida

[1] Certain fresh waters of Calhoun, Gulf and Jackson Counties are closed to fishing during April and May. (See Chapter 16.)